PERSONAL FINANCE HANDBOOK

YOUR ESSENTIAL GUIDE TO FINANCIAL FREEDOM AND SECURITY

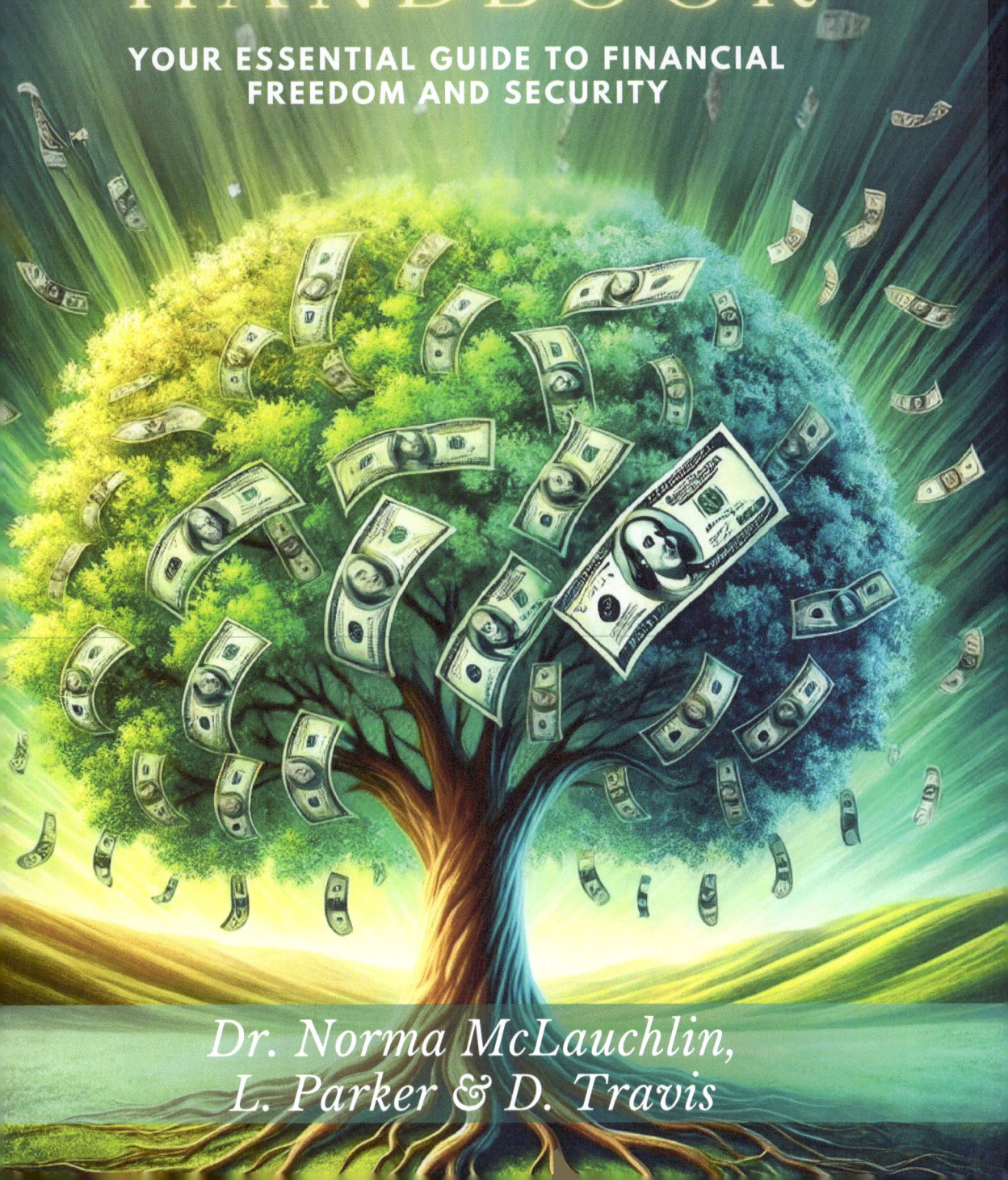

Dr. Norma McLauchlin, L. Parker & D. Travis

PERSONAL FINANCE HANDBOOK
YOUR ESSENTIAL GUIDE TO FINANCIAL FREEDOM AND SECURITY

ISBN: 978-1-966163-03-9
Personal Finance Handbook
'Your Essential Guide to Financial Freedom and Security'
Categories:
Self-Help / Success
- Personal Finance
- Investing / Beginner's Guides
Entrepreneurship / Financial Planning
Education / Financial Literacy

Published by:

To order additional copies of the resource, write customer service:
1420 Hoke Loop Road
Fayetteville, NC 28314
FAX orders to 910-868-3300
Phone orders to 910-818-6652

Printed in the United States of America
10 9 8 7 6 5 4 3 2 1
Front cover image by Joyce Licorish - DreamEmpire Publishing
Book design by Joyce Licorish - DreamEmpire Publishing
Printed by - Amazon | Ingram Spark
First printing edition September 2024

For Author Appearances or Bookings visit:
www.ChosePen.com
contact@chosepen.com
910.758.1811

DEDICATION

To all those striving for financial stability and independence. May this handbook serve as a beacon of guidance on your journey to financial empowerment.

TABLE OF CONTENTS

A WORD FROM THE AUTHORS

Dear Reader,

Thank you for choosing the *Personal Finance Handbook*, our mission is to provide you with practical knowledge and actionable steps to enhance your financial well-being. This handbook is a culmination of years of research, experience, and a passion for helping others achieve financial success. I hope you find the information valuable and inspiring as you embark on your journey toward financial freedom.

Dr. Norma McLauchlin,
 L. Parker & D. Travis

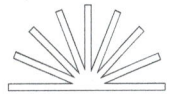

THANKS!

"An investment in knowledge pays the best interest." - Benjamin Franklin

GETTING STARTED

In today's complex financial landscape, understanding personal finance is more important than ever. With the right knowledge and tools, you can take charge of your financial future, make informed decisions, and work towards achieving your financial goals. The *Personal Finance Handbook* is designed to provide you with a comprehensive overview of essential financial concepts, strategies, and best practices. This handbook will guide you through various aspects of personal finance, including budgeting, saving, investing, and understanding your rights as a consumer.

QUESTIONS?

Write: 1420 Hoke Loop Road
Fayetteville, NC 28314

Email: contact@chosepen.com

CHAPTER ONE

UNDERSTANDING PERSONAL FINANCE

What is Personal Finance?

Personal finance encompasses the management of an individual's financial activities, including budgeting, saving, investing, and planning for future financial goals. It is not just about handling money but also about making informed decisions that align with one's values and aspirations. Personal finance is a lifelong journey that requires knowledge, discipline, and the ability to adapt to changing circumstances.

Explanation: *Understanding personal finance is essential for achieving financial stability and independence. It helps individuals navigate their financial lives effectively, ensuring they can meet current needs while planning for future goals.*

The Importance of Personal Finance

Understanding personal finance is vital for several reasons:

- Financial Security: Mastering personal finance provides a foundation for financial security, reducing stress and anxiety related to money matters.
- Goal Achievement: With proper planning, individuals can set and achieve specific financial goals, such as homeownership, education funding, or retirement savings.
- Wealth Building: Knowledge of personal finance equips individuals with the tools needed to build wealth over time through strategic saving and investing.

Key components of Personal Finance include:

- Budgeting: Creating a spending plan to allocate income toward expenses, savings, and investments. A budget helps individuals prioritize their financial goals and manage their cash flow effectively.

- Saving: Setting aside money for emergencies, future purchases, and retirement. Saving is essential for financial security and allows individuals to reach their goals without relying on debt.

- Investing: Allocating funds to assets that can grow in value over time. Investing is crucial for building wealth and outpacing inflation, allowing individuals to achieve long-term financial goals.

- Debt Management: Understanding, controlling, and repaying personal debt. Effective debt management prevents financial strain and maintains a healthy credit profile.

Each component of personal finance plays a critical role in an individual's financial health. Understanding how these elements interconnect enables individuals to create a comprehensive financial strategy.

Setting Financial Goals

Setting financial goals involves:

- Types of Goals: Categorizing goals into short-term, medium-term, and long-term. Short-term goals might include saving for a vacation, medium term goals might include paying back student loans, while long-term goals could involve retirement planning.

- Set SMART Goals:

What Are SMART Goals?

SMART goals provide a proven framework for setting clear, realistic, and actionable financial objectives. Each element ensures your goals are specific, achievable, and trackable, increasing your chances of financial success.

How to Set SMART Financial Goals

1. Specific

Clearly define what you want to achieve in your finances. Answer: Who? What? Where? When? Why?

- Example: Instead of "Save money," specify: "Save $10,000 for a home down payment."

2. Measurable

Set criteria to track your progress and determine success.

- Example: Refine to: "Save $10,000 by setting aside $500 per month."

3. Achievable

Ensure your goal is realistic given your income, expenses, and resources.

- Example: Adjust: "Save $10,000 over two years by cutting discretionary spending and increasing side income."

4. Relevant/Realistic

In the SMART goals framework, "Relevant" and "Realistic" are often used interchangeably to represent the "R." A goal is Relevant when it aligns with broader objectives, ensuring it contributes meaningfully to overarching plans. It is Realistic when it is attainable within available resources and constraints, making it practical and achievable. Both aspects are crucial for setting effective goals that are both meaningful and feasible.

Align your goal with your overall financial priorities and life plans.

- Example: "Saving for a home down payment aligns with my goal of buying a house in two years."

5. Time-bound

Set a clear deadline to stay motivated and focused.

- Example: "Save $10,000 within 24 months."

Benefits of Setting SMART Financial Goals

- Clarity & Focus: Clearly defined goals prevent overspending and encourage saving.
- Trackable Progress: Monitor your financial journey and stay on track.
- Realistic Planning: Ensure your goals align with your financial situation.
- Time Management: Deadlines create urgency and help prioritize spending.

SETTING GOALS THE S.M.A.R.T. WAY

SPECIFIC

MEASUREABLE

ACHIEVABLE

RELEVANT

TIMEBOUND

"Clear goals lead to confident actions—SMART planning turns dreams into reality."

DR. NORMA MCLAUCHLIN

Other Great Ways to Set and Manage Your Financial Goals:
- Visualizing Goals: Utilizing vision boards or digital tools to visualize goals can enhance motivation and commitment. This practice helps reinforce the importance of achieving these financial objectives.

Setting clear financial goals provides direction and motivation. It helps individuals prioritize their financial efforts and stay focused on their long-term aspirations.

Importance of Tracking Progress

Tracking progress involves
- Regular Check-Ins: Scheduling monthly reviews to assess financial situations, including budgets and savings. This practice helps identify areas for improvement and reinforces accountability.

- Utilizing Technology: Leveraging financial tracking apps to monitor expenses, savings, and investments in real-time. Technology can simplify tracking and provide insights into spending habits.

- Accountability Partners: Sharing financial goals with a trusted friend or family member can create a support system, encouraging accountability and motivation.

Monitoring progress is essential for staying on track to achieve financial goals. It allows individuals to make necessary adjustments and celebrate milestones along the way.

6 MONEY TIPS
For Managing Personal Finances

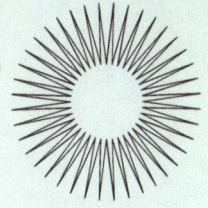

✓ **Create a Budget and Stick to It** - A budget helps you understand where your money is going and ensures you prioritize your spending.

✓ **Build an Emergency Fund** - Life is unpredictable, and an emergency fund can prevent financial stress during unexpected events like medical emergencies or job loss.

✓ **Pay Off Debt Strategically** - Debt can hinder financial growth and add stress to your life.

✓ **Invest in Your Future** - Investing helps grow your wealth and prepare for long-term goals like retirement or buying a home.

✓ **Live Below Your Means** - Spending less than you earn allows you to save and invest more, creating financial security.

✓ **Continuously Educate Yourself About Finances** - Financial literacy is essential for making informed decisions and maximizing your wealth. You are on the right track by reading this book to further educate yourself about how to improve your personal finances.

Comprehension
Q&A

Reflect on what you've learned in this chapter by answering the following questions.

Q1 Define personal finance and explain its significance in your daily life.

Q2 List the key components of personal finance and provide a brief description of each.

Q3 Why is it essential to track your financial activities regularly?

Q4 Explain how budgeting can lead to better financial decision-making.

Q5 Provide an example of how personal finance concepts can affect long-term financial goals.

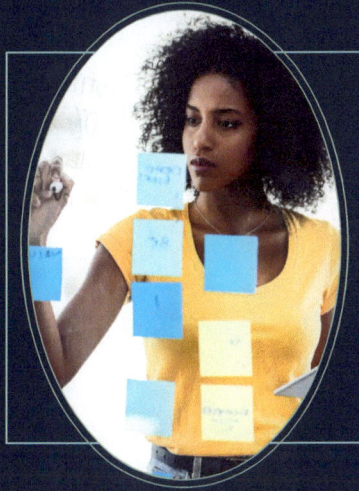

CHAPTER TWO
SETTING FINANCIAL GOALS

2.1 Understanding Financial Goals

Financial goals are specific targets that guide financial planning. They can range from short-term objectives, like saving for a new phone, to long-term aspirations, such as retirement savings. Setting financial goals provides clarity and motivation, helping individuals focus their efforts on what is most important.

Explanation: Financial goals act as a roadmap for financial decision-making. By setting clear, actionable targets, individuals can make informed choices that align with their overall financial strategy.

2.2 Types of Financial Goals
- *Short-Term Goals: Goals aimed to be achieved within a year, such as saving for a vacation or paying off a small debt. These goals require immediate attention and planning.*

- Medium-Term Goals: Goals typically spanning one to five years, such as saving for a down payment on a home or funding a child's education. These goals may require more substantial savings efforts and careful planning.
- Long-Term Goals: Goals that take more than five years to achieve, such as retirement planning or building a substantial investment portfolio. Long-term goals often require a comprehensive financial plan that includes regular investments and savings.

Explanation: Understanding the varying timeframes for goals allows individuals to prioritize their financial resources effectively. Each type of goal requires different strategies and resources.

2.3 The Role of Emergency Funds
Emergency funds are essential for financial stability. They act as a safety net during unexpected financial challenges, such as job loss or medical emergencies. Having three to six months of living expenses saved can provide peace of mind and help prevent reliance on credit.

Explanation: An emergency fund protects individuals from financial setbacks. It allows for better financial decision-making during crises, reducing stress and promoting resilience.

2.4 Adjusting Goals Over Time
Life circumstances can change, necessitating adjustments to financial goals. Major life changes, such as marriage or having children, can impact financial situations and priorities. Regularly reassessing goals ensures they remain relevant and achievable.

Explanation: Flexibility in financial planning is crucial. By adapting to life changes and economic conditions, individuals can maintain progress toward their goals despite challenges.

Comprehension
Q&A

Reflect on what you've learned in this chapter by answering the following questions.

Q1 What are financial goals, and why are they important?

Q2 Differentiate between short-term, medium-term, and long-term financial goals.

Q3 How can setting specific financial goals impact your spending habits?

Q4 Discuss the SMART criteria for setting effective financial goals.

Q5 Provide an example of a financial goal you would like to set and outline the steps to achieve it.

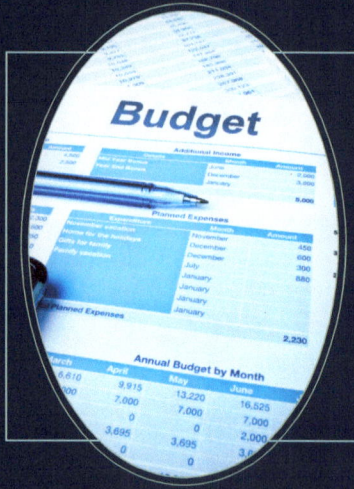

CHAPTER THREE

BUDGETING BASICS

3.1 What is a Budget?

A budget is a financial plan that outlines expected income and expenses over a specific period. It provides a framework for managing money, allowing individuals to track spending, save for goals, and avoid debt.

Explanation: Creating a budget is fundamental to financial management. It helps individuals allocate resources effectively and make informed decisions about their finances.

3.2 Importance of Budgeting

Budgeting is crucial for several reasons:

- Financial Control: A budget allows individuals to track spending and manage their finances effectively. It provides insight into where money is going and helps identify areas for improvement.

- Goal Achievement: A clear budget allocates funds toward financial goals, ensuring individuals stay on track. It helps prioritize spending and savings in alignment with personal objectives.
- Avoiding Debt: Budgeting can prevent overspending, reducing the risk of accumulating debt. By knowing spending limits, individuals can prioritize essential expenses and avoid unnecessary purchases.

Explanation: Budgeting promotes responsible financial behavior. It encourages individuals to make intentional choices about how they spend and save money.

3.3 Creating a Budget
To create a budget, follow these steps:
1. Determine Income: Calculate total monthly income from all sources, including salary, side gigs, and investment income.
2. List Expenses: Identify all monthly expenses, including fixed (rent, utilities) and variable (groceries, entertainment) costs. Being thorough ensures accurate budgeting.
3. Set Spending Limits: Allocate specific amounts to each expense category based on income and financial goals. This helps prioritize essential expenses while allowing for discretionary spending.
4. Monitor and Adjust: Regularly track spending and adjust the budget as needed to stay on track. Review monthly to identify trends and areas for improvement.

Explanation: Creating a budget requires careful consideration of income and expenses. A well-structured budget provides a clear path toward achieving financial goals.

3.4 Budgeting Methods

Several budgeting methods can help individuals manage finances:

- Zero-Based Budgeting: Allocate every dollar of income to specific expenses, savings, or debt repayment, ensuring that income minus expenses equals zero.

- 50/30/20 Rule: Allocate 50% of income to needs, 30% to wants, and 20% to savings and debt repayment. This simple method provides a straightforward approach to budgeting.

- Envelope System: Use envelopes to separate cash for different spending categories. Once the money in an envelope is gone, spending in that category stops. This method promotes discipline and accountability in spending.

Comprehension
Q&A

Reflect on what you've learned in this chapter by answering the following questions.

Q1   Explain the importance of having a budget.

Q2   What are the key elements of a budget?

Q3   How does budgeting help in achieving financial goals?

Q4   Discuss the difference between fixed and variable expenses with examples.

Q5   Describe a budgeting method that you find effective and explain why.

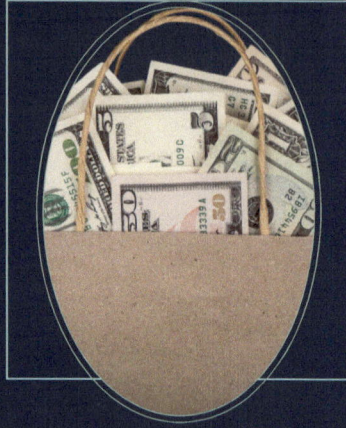

CHAPTER FOUR
INCOME SOURCES

4.1 Types of Income

Understanding different types of income is essential for effective financial management:

1. Earned Income: Money earned through employment, including wages and bonuses. This is often the primary source of income for most individuals and is subject to income tax.

2. Investment Income: Earnings generated from investments, such as dividends, interest, or capital gains. This type of income can vary based on market performance and investment choices.

3. Passive Income: Income derived from investments or business ventures requiring minimal effort to maintain. Examples include rental income, royalties, and dividends from stocks.

Explanation: Diversifying income sources can provide greater financial security and stability. Understanding the types of income allows individuals to explore opportunities for increasing earnings.

4.2 Exploring Multiple Income Streams

Diversifying income sources can provide financial security:
- Side Gigs: Consider taking on part-time jobs or freelance work to supplement primary income. Popular options include consulting, freelance writing, or driving for ride-sharing services.
- Investing: Allocate funds to investment accounts to generate passive income over time. This could involve investing in stocks, bonds, or real estate, which can yield returns beyond traditional savings.

Explanation: Relying solely on one income source can be risky. Exploring multiple income streams can enhance financial resilience and provide additional opportunities for wealth creation.

4.3 Maximizing Your Income Potential

Maximizing income is essential for achieving financial goals:
- Skill Development: Invest in skill development through courses or certifications that can lead to promotions or higher-paying job opportunities. Continuous learning can enhance marketability.
- Networking: Build a professional network that can lead to new job opportunities or side gigs. Networking can provide valuable connections and insights into potential career advancements.

Explanation: Investing in personal and professional growth can lead to increased income potential. Building a network can also provide support and resources for career development.

Comprehension
Q&A

Reflect on what you've learned in this chapter by answering the following questions.

Q1   Define earned income and provide two examples.

Q2   What is passive income, and how can it be generated?

Q3   Discuss the importance of diversifying income sources.

Q4   How can investments contribute to your overall income?

Q5   Provide an example of a side hustle that could generate additional income.

CHAPTER FIVE
FINANCIAL DECISION-MAKING

5.1 The Process of Financial Decision-Making

Financial decision-making involves evaluating options and making choices that impact financial well-being. A systematic approach enhances decision-making skills:

1. Identify the Decision: Clearly define the financial decision to be made, whether budgeting, investing, or purchasing a significant item.

2. Gather Information: Research and gather relevant data about available options, including prices, features, and benefits.

3. Evaluate Alternatives: Assess the pros and cons of each option, considering factors such as costs, benefits, and risks.

4. Make a Decision: Choose the option that aligns best with financial goals and values.

5. Monitor Results: After making a decision, monitor outcomes and adjust approaches as needed. Reflecting on what worked and what didn't can improve future decision-making.

Explanation: A structured decision-making process allows individuals to make informed choices that align with their financial goals and values. It promotes confidence and reduces the likelihood of regret.

5.2 Evaluating Financial Decisions

When making financial decisions, consider:

- Cost-Benefit Analysis: Assess potential costs and benefits to determine overall value. For example, when deciding whether to buy a new car, evaluate purchase price, maintenance costs, and fuel efficiency.
- Scenario Planning: Anticipate different scenarios and their potential outcomes. This approach allows for preparation for various possibilities and informed decision-making.

Explanation: Evaluating financial decisions ensures that choices are grounded in logic and reason. It encourages individuals to think critically about their options.

5.3 The Role of Emotions in Financial Decision-Making

Emotions can significantly influence financial decisions:

- Mindfulness Techniques: Practice mindfulness techniques, such as meditation, to help calm emotional reactions during decision-making. Remaining calm can lead to more rational choices.
- Avoid Impulsive Decisions: Allow time for reflection before making significant purchases. Implement a waiting period of 24-48 hours to avoid impulse buying.

Explanation: Recognizing the impact of emotions on financial decisions can help individuals make more rational choices. Mindfulness and patience can reduce the likelihood of regrettable.

5.4 Seeking Professional Advice (continued)

- Investment Professionals: If considering investing, seek advice from investment professionals who can provide tailored strategies based on risk tolerance and financial goals. They can help you navigate investment options and market conditions, ensuring your investment choices align with your long-term objectives.

Explanation: Professional financial advice can provide valuable insights and guidance, helping individuals make informed decisions that align with their financial goals. Financial advisors can help simplify complex concepts and offer strategies that may not be apparent to novice investors.

Comprehension
Q&A

Reflect on what you've learned in this chapter by answering the following questions.

01 Describe the steps involved in the financial decision-making process.

02 Why is it important to weigh the pros and cons of financial decisions?

03 How can emotional factors influence financial decision-making?

04 Discuss the role of research in making informed financial decisions.

05 Provide an example of a financial decision you made and the process you followed.

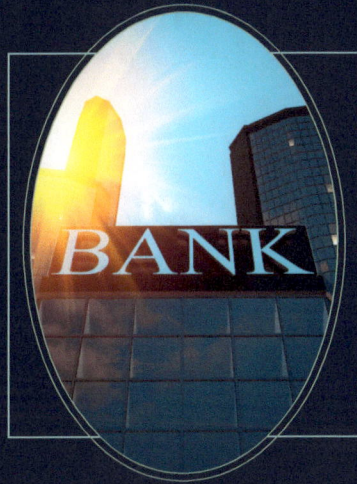

CHAPTER SIX

BANKING BASICS

6.1 Types of Banking Institutions

Understanding different types of banking institutions can help you choose the right one for your needs:

1. Commercial Banks: Offer a wide range of financial services, including checking and savings accounts, loans, and mortgages. They typically have physical branches and online services, providing convenience for customers.

2. Credit Unions: Non-profit organizations that provide banking services to members, often with lower fees and better interest rates. Membership is usually based on a common affiliation, such as a workplace or community.

3. Online Banks: Banks that operate entirely online, typically offering higher interest rates on savings accounts due to lower overhead costs. They may lack physical branches but often provide user-friendly digital services.

Explanation: Understanding the different types of banking institutions allows individuals to select the one that best meets their financial needs, preferences, and goals. Each type has distinct advantages and disadvantages.

6.2 Choosing the Right Bank

Selecting the right bank involves considering several factors:
- Fees and Charges: Research the fees associated with different banks, such as monthly maintenance fees, ATM fees, and overdraft charges. Opt for banks with minimal fees that align with your financial needs.
- Customer Service: Evaluate customer service ratings for banks. Look for institutions with positive reviews regarding customer support, as this can significantly impact your banking experience.

Explanation: Choosing the right bank is an important decision that can affect everyday financial activities. Ensuring that the bank aligns with your needs and values can lead to a more satisfying banking experience.

6.3 Understanding Bank Products

Familiarize yourself with various bank products to make informed choices:
- Checking Accounts: Essential for daily transactions; look for accounts with no monthly fees and convenient access to ATMs. Some accounts may offer additional features like overdraft protection or rewards for usage.
- Savings Accounts: A safe place to store money while earning interest. Research accounts with competitive interest rates and no minimum balance requirements for better savings growth.
- Certificates of Deposit (CDs): Time deposits that offer higher interest rates than regular savings accounts. Understand the terms and penalties for early withdrawal when considering CDs.

Explanation: Understanding bank products is critical for effective money management. Each product serves a specific purpose and can contribute to achieving overall financial goals.

6.4 Utilizing Online Banking Tools

Online banking offers various tools that can enhance financial management:

- Mobile Banking Apps: Many banks have mobile apps that allow you to manage your accounts, transfer funds, and pay bills on the go. These apps often provide real-time notifications for transactions, enhancing convenience.
- Budgeting Tools: Some banks offer budgeting tools that help you track spending and set financial goals directly within your banking platform. These tools can integrate with your accounts for a comprehensive view of your finances.

Explanation: Leveraging online banking tools can simplify financial management. These tools provide accessibility and resources that can aid in budgeting and tracking financial activities.

6.5 Understanding Interest Rates

Interest rates impact savings and borrowing:

- Variable vs. Fixed Rates: Understand the difference between variable and fixed interest rates. Fixed rates remain constant, while variable rates can fluctuate based on market conditions, affecting loan repayments and savings growth.
- APY vs. APR: Familiarize yourself with Annual Percentage Yield (APY) for savings accounts and Annual Percentage Rate (APR) for loans. APY reflects the total interest earned on a savings account, while APR indicates the cost of borrowing.

Explanation: Understanding interest rates is fundamental for managing loans and savings. It helps individuals make informed decisions about borrowing and investing.

6.6 Check Writing: A Traditional Skill in Modern Finance

In today's digital age, the art of check writing may seem outdated, yet it remains an essential skill in personal finance. Understanding how to write a check not only empowers you to manage your finances effectively but also provides a secure method of payment for various transactions, such as paying rent, settling invoices, or gifting money. This section will guide you through the steps of writing a check, best practices, and alternatives to consider.

How to Write a Check: Step-by-Step Instructions
1. Date the Check
Begin by writing the current date in the top right corner. This identifies when the check was issued and is crucial for record-keeping.

Example: If you are writing a check on April 15, 2023, you would write:

04/15/2023

2. Payee Name:

On the line that begins with "Pay to the Order of," write the name of the person or organization you are paying. Ensure the spelling is correct to avoid any issues with cashing the check.

Example: If you are paying your landlord, write:

Pay to the Order of: John Smith

3. Amount in Numbers

In the box next to the payee's name, write the amount you are paying in numerical form (e.g., "150.75"). Be careful to leave no space between the numbers and the box to prevent alterations.
Example: For a payment of $1,200, write:

$1,200.00

4. Amount in Words
Below the payee name, write the amount in words (e.g., "One hundred fifty and 75/100"). This acts as a second verification of the amount and is critical in case there is a dispute.
Example: For the above payment of $1,200, you would write:

One thousand two hundred and 00/100 dollars

5. Memo Line
Use the memo line to note the purpose of the payment (e.g., "April Rent" or "Grocery Shopping"). This can help you and the payee keep track of what the payment is for.
Example:
If the payment is for rent, write:

Memo: April Rent

6. Signature

Sign the check on the line at the bottom right. Your signature authorizes the payment, so it must match the signature on file with your bank.
Example: Sign your name as you would on any official document:

Your Name

Sample Check:
Here's an example of a filled-out check:

Date: 04/15/2023

Pay to the Order of: John Smith
$ 1,200.00

One thousand two hundred and 00/100 dollars

Memo: April Rent

Signature: [Your Signature]

Tips and Best Practices
- Keep Checks Secure: Store your checks in a safe place to prevent theft or fraud. Consider using a locked drawer or a safe.

- Track Your Payments: Maintain a check register to record each check written. Note the date, payee, amount, and purpose. This helps keep track of your spending and ensures you do not overspend.

Example Check Register Entry:
Date: 04/15/2023
Check Number: 101
Payee: John Smith
Amount: $1,200.00
Memo: April Rent
Balance: $3,800.00 (after payment)

Be Aware of Bounced Checks

Writing a check without sufficient funds can lead to overdraft fees and potential legal issues. Always ensure you have enough money in your account to cover the check.

Practical Exercises
To practice your check-writing skills, try filling out the following scenarios:

Scenario 1: You are paying your monthly rent of $1,200. Write a check for this amount, including the date and memo.
- Solution: Follow the steps outlined above to fill out the check.

Scenario 2: You bought groceries totaling $75.50 at the supermarket.

Example Check:
- Date: 04/20/2023
- Pay to the Order of: Supermarket XYZ
- $75.50
- Seventy-five and 50/100 dollars
- Memo: Groceries
- Signature: [Your Name]

Scenario 3: You hired a plumber for a repair job that cost $250.

Example Check:
- Date: 04/25/2023
- Pay to the Order of: Joe's Plumbing
- $250.00
- Two hundred fifty and 00/100 dollars
- Memo: Plumbing Repair
- Signature: [Your Name]

Alternatives to Check Writing

While checks are still useful, digital payment methods such as online banking and mobile payment apps have become increasingly popular. Consider the following pros and cons:

- Checks:
  - Pros: Provide a paper trail, secure for certain transactions, can be mailed or delivered in person.
  - Cons: Can be lost or stolen, may require manual tracking, and may take longer to clear.
- Digital Payments:
  - Pros: Fast, convenient, often automated, and can be managed from a mobile device or computer.
  - Cons: May lack the same level of security if not properly managed, and some people may find it harder to track spending without a physical record.

Conclusion

Mastering the skill of check writing is a valuable addition to your financial toolkit. It enhances your ability to manage payments securely and helps you maintain control over your finances. Take the time to practice this skill, and consider when it may be appropriate to use checks versus digital payment methods in your everyday transactions.

Your name _____   0123

Date _____ 20 ___

Pay to the order of _____

_____ dollars

$ _____

Security features included details on back

Memo _____ _____

:012345678 :0123 :01234

Comprehension
Q&A

Reflect on what you've learned in this chapter by answering the following questions.

01 Compare and contrast commercial banks and credit unions.

02 What factors should you consider when choosing a bank?

03 Explain the significance of understanding bank products.

04 How do online banking tools facilitate personal finance management?

05 Describe the difference between APY and APR and their relevance to savings and loans.

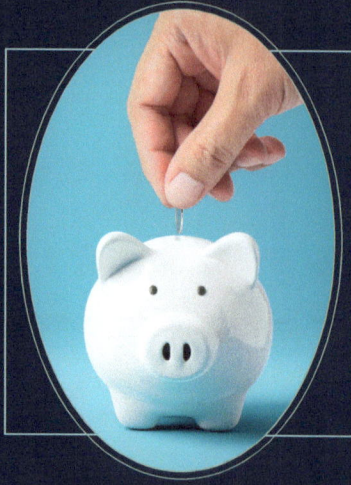

CHAPTER SEVEN
SAVING STRATEGIES

7.1 The Importance of Saving

Saving money is a fundamental aspect of financial health. It provides a safety net for emergencies and helps achieve financial goals. Developing a strong saving habit can lead to greater financial stability and reduce reliance on credit.

Explanation: Saving is crucial for both short-term needs and long-term financial security. It allows individuals to prepare for unexpected expenses and achieve their financial aspirations without going into debt.

7.2 Types of Savings Accounts

Different savings accounts serve various purposes:

1. Regular Savings Accounts: Basic accounts offered by banks and credit unions that typically provide lower interest rates. These accounts are suitable for short-term savings and liquidity.

2. High-Yield Savings Accounts: Accounts that offer higher interest rates than traditional savings accounts, often available through online banks. These accounts are ideal for building savings while earning more interest.

3. Money Market Accounts: Savings accounts that typically offer higher interest rates and allow limited check-writing capabilities. These accounts may require a higher minimum balance.

Explanation: Understanding the types of savings accounts available allows individuals to select the option that best fits their saving goals and strategies.

7.3 Establishing a Savings Plan

A well-defined savings plan can enhance your ability to save effectively:

- Set Clear Savings Goals: Define specific savings goals, such as building an emergency fund or saving for a vacation. Knowing what you're saving for can motivate you to set aside money regularly.

- Determine Savings Amounts: Decide how much money you can realistically save each month based on your budget. Start with a manageable amount and gradually increase it as your financial situation improves.

Explanation: Establishing a savings plan provides structure and direction, making it easier to achieve specific financial goals. It encourages disciplined saving habits.

7.4 Automatic Savings

Automating savings can simplify the process and promote consistency:

- Automatic Transfers: Arrange for automatic transfers from your checking account to your savings account on payday. This "pay yourself first" approach ensures that you prioritize savings before spending.

- Employer-Sponsored Savings Plans: If available, consider participating in employer-sponsored savings plans, such as direct deposit into a savings account or retirement plan. This can streamline the saving process.

Explanation: Automating savings removes the temptation to spend money that should be saved. It promotes a consistent saving habit, making it easier to reach financial goals.

7.5 Utilizing Savings Tools

Leverage various tools to enhance your saving efforts:

- High-Yield Savings Accounts: Research high-yield savings accounts that offer better interest rates than traditional savings accounts. This can help your savings grow more effectively over time.

- Savings Challenges: Engage in savings challenges, such as the 52-week savings challenge, to make saving fun and motivating. Participate with friends or family for additional accountability.

7.6 Setting Up an Emergency Fund

An emergency fund is crucial for financial stability:

- Determine the Amount Needed: Aim to save three to six months' worth of living expenses in your emergency fund. This amount provides a cushion for unforeseen circumstances.

- Separate Savings Account: Keep your emergency fund in a separate savings account to avoid the temptation to dip into it for non-emergencies. This helps ensure the funds are readily available when needed.

Explanation: An emergency fund acts as a financial buffer, providing security and peace of mind during unexpected situations. It allows individuals to handle emergencies without accumulating debt.

Comprehension
Q&A

Reflect on what you've learned in this chapter by answering the following questions.

Q1   Why is saving important for achieving financial security?

Q2   What are some common saving strategies?

Q3   Discuss the difference between short-term and long-term savings goals.

Q4   How can automatic savings help individuals save more effectively?

Q5   Provide an example of a specific savings goal you have set for yourself.

8.2 Importance of Credit

Understanding credit is essential for several reasons:
- Purchasing Power: Good credit enables access to loans, credit cards, and mortgages, allowing individuals to make significant purchases and investments.
- Favorable Terms: A higher credit score can lead to lower interest rates and better loan terms, saving money over time. Understanding how to maintain a good credit score is crucial for financial health.
- Financial Opportunities: Good credit can open doors to opportunities, such as renting an apartment or securing employment in certain industries. Many landlords and employers check credit reports during the application process.

Explanation: Credit is a critical aspect of personal finance that can significantly impact an individual's financial opportunities and costs. Understanding credit management is essential for achieving financial goals.

8.3 Types of Credit

1. Revolving Credit: Credit that allows you to borrow up to a certain limit and repay it over time, such as credit cards. This type of credit offers flexibility but can lead to debt if not managed properly.

2. Installment Credit: Loans with fixed repayment schedules, such as personal loans, auto loans, or mortgages. These loans typically have a set interest rate and payment amount, making budgeting easier.

3. Open Credit: Credit accounts that require full payment each month, such as charge cards. These accounts do not allow carrying a balance, which can help avoid debt accumulation.

Explanation: Understanding the different types of credit allows individuals to choose the right credit products for their needs. Each type has unique features and implications for financial management.

8.4 Building a Positive Credit History

Establishing a positive credit history is essential for long-term financial health:

- Start with a Secured Credit Card: If you're new to credit or have a low credit score, consider obtaining a secured credit card. This type of card requires a cash deposit as collateral, which serves as your credit limit. By using the card responsibly and making timely payments, you can build a positive credit history over time.

- Make Payments on Time: Your payment history is one of the most significant factors affecting your credit score. Consistently making on-time payments demonstrates reliability to creditors and can boost your credit score. Set up reminders or automate payments to avoid missed deadlines.

- Keep Credit Utilization Low: Credit utilization refers to the ratio of your credit card balances to your credit limits. Aim to keep your utilization below 30%. For example, if you have a credit limit of $1,000, try to keep your balance below $300. High utilization can negatively impact your credit score.

Explanation: Building a positive credit history is crucial for accessing favorable borrowing terms in the future. Responsible credit management fosters trust with lenders and enhances overall financial opportunities.

8.5 Monitoring Your Credit Score

Regularly monitoring your credit score can help you stay informed about your credit health:

- Free Credit Reports: Take advantage of your right to obtain free credit reports annually from the three major credit bureaus. Review your reports for accuracy and dispute any errors promptly.

- Credit Monitoring Services: Consider using credit monitoring services that provide real-time alerts for changes to your credit report. This can help you stay on top of your credit health and detect potential fraud.

- Understanding Credit Scoring Models: Familiarize yourself with common credit scoring models, such as FICO and VantageScore. These models assess different factors, including payment history, credit utilization, length of credit history, types of credit accounts, and recent credit inquiries.

Explanation: Monitoring your credit score enables proactive management of your financial health. It helps identify areas for improvement and allows you to take corrective actions before issues arise.

Comprehension
Q&A

Reflect on what you've learned in this chapter by answering the following questions.

01 Define credit and explain its importance in personal finance.

02 What are the different types of credit available to consumers?

03 Discuss how to build and maintain a positive credit history.

04 Why is it essential to monitor your credit score regularly?

05 Explain the factors that influence your credit score and how to manage them.

CHAPTER EIGHT
UNDERSTANDING CREDIT

8.1 Understanding Credit

Credit is the power to access money, goods, or services now — with the agreement that you'll pay later. It's more than a financial tool; it's a relationship built on trust between you and lenders. When used wisely, credit can open doors to opportunities like buying a home, financing a car, or investing in education.

Leveraging credit means using it to your advantage — not just borrowing, but borrowing smart. It requires understanding how credit works, how interest accumulates, and how your actions today affect your financial future. Responsible credit use can help you build a strong financial foundation, while misuse can lead to debt and long-term financial stress.

Use credit as a stepping stone, not a crutch. With the right strategy, you can turn credit into a powerful asset on your journey to financial freedom

8.2 Credit = Building Your Financial Reputation

Credit is more than just a score — it's a reflection of how you manage debt and financial responsibility. In this chapter, you'll learn what credit is, how it works, and why it matters. From credit reports to interest rates and utilization, we'll break down the essentials to help you build and maintain healthy credit. Empower yourself to make smart decisions and take control of your financial future.

Top 10 Tips for Building Good Credit

1. **Pay Your Bills on Time – Every Time**
Your payment history makes up the largest portion of your credit score. Set reminders or automate payments to stay consistent.

2. **Keep Credit Card Balances Low**
Aim to use less than 30% of your available credit limit — ideally under 10% for the best results.

3. **Don't Close Old Accounts**
The length of your credit history matters. Keeping older accounts open (even if unused) can boost your score.

4. **Only Apply for Credit When Necessary**
Too many credit inquiries in a short time can hurt your score. Be selective and strategic.

5. **Check Your Credit Reports Regularly**
Monitor your credit reports for errors or fraud. You're entitled to one free report per year from each of the three major bureaus via AnnualCreditReport.com.

6. **Dispute Errors Promptly**
Mistakes can drag your score down. If you find inaccuracies, report them immediately and follow up until they're resolved.

7. **Diversify Your Credit Mix**
A healthy mix of credit types (like a credit card, auto loan, or student loan) shows lenders you can manage different forms of debt.

8. **Become an Authorized User**
Being added to someone else's well-managed credit card account can help build your credit history — just be sure they use credit responsibly.

9. **Keep New Accounts to a Minimum**
New accounts lower your average credit age and can temporarily drop your score. Space out new applications wisely.

10. **Create a Budget and Stick to It**
Sound money management prevents missed payments and high balances — two major credit score killers.

Comprehension
Q&A

Reflect on what you've learned in this chapter by answering the following questions.

Q1 What does having "good credit" mean, and why is it important?

Q2 What factors impact your credit score the most?

Q3 How can credit card usage help or hurt your credit?

Q4 What are three specific actions you can take this month to improve or protect your credit?

Q5 How would you explain credit to a teenager in one or two sentences?

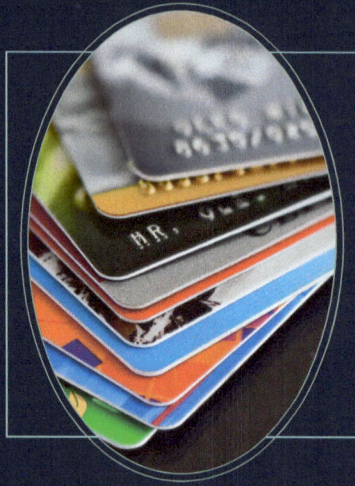

CHAPTER NINE

MANAGING DEBT

9.1 Understanding Debt

Debt is money borrowed that must be repaid, often with interest. It can be classified into two main categories:

- Good Debt: Debt that is considered beneficial, such as student loans or mortgages, which can lead to increased income or asset ownership. Good debt can be an investment in your future and may enhance your financial situation over time.

- Bad Debt: Debt incurred from high-interest loans, such as credit card debt, which can lead to financial strain. Bad debt typically does not contribute to asset building and can create a cycle of borrowing that is difficult to escape.

Explanation: Understanding the difference between good and bad debt is essential for effective financial management. It allows individuals to make informed borrowing decisions that align with their long-term financial goals.

9.2 The Impact of Debt on Finances

Managing debt is crucial for maintaining financial health. Here are some impacts of debt:

- Interest Payments: Debt often comes with interest, which can accumulate over time and increase the total amount owed. Understanding how interest works is vital for managing debt effectively. For example, high-interest credit card debt can quickly spiral out of control if not addressed.
- Credit Score Effects: High levels of debt can negatively impact your credit score, making it harder to obtain favorable loan terms in the future. Maintaining a low debt-to-income ratio is essential for a healthy credit profile.
- Financial Stress: Carrying significant debt can lead to financial stress and anxiety, impacting overall well-being. Strategies such as budgeting, debt repayment plans, and seeking financial advice can help alleviate this stress and regain control over your finances.

Explanation: Recognizing the impact of debt on overall financial health can motivate individuals to take proactive measures to manage and reduce debt effectively.

9.3 Strategies for Debt Management

Effective debt management is crucial for financial health:

1. Create a Debt Repayment Plan: Outline how much to pay each month toward each debt. Prioritize debts with the highest interest rates for efficient repayment. The snowball method (paying off the smallest debts first) and avalanche method (paying off the highest interest debts first) are popular strategies.
2. Prioritize High-Interest Debt: Focus on paying off debts with the highest interest rates first (the avalanche method) or tackle the smallest debts first for quick wins (the snowball method). Both strategies have their merits, and choosing one depends on personal preference and motivation.

3. Consider Debt Consolidation: Combining multiple debts into a single loan can lower interest rates and simplify payments. However, ensure that the terms are favorable and consider potential fees. Debt consolidation can be a useful tool for those struggling to manage multiple payments.

Explanation: Implementing effective debt management strategies can help individuals regain control over their finances and work toward becoming debt-free.

9.4 Creating a Debt Repayment Plan

A debt repayment plan provides structure and clarity:

1. List All Debts: Include total amounts owed, interest rates, and minimum payments. This comprehensive list will guide your repayment strategy.

2. Set a Payment Schedule: Determine how much you can allocate to each debt monthly. Ensure that you meet at least the minimum payments on all debts.

3. Monitor Progress: Regularly review your debt repayment progress. Celebrate milestones, such as paying off a debt, to stay motivated and focused.

9.5 Overcoming Debt Challenges

Managing debt can be challenging, but with the right strategies, you can overcome obstacles:

- Avoiding New Debt: It's essential to avoid accumulating new debt while focusing on repayment. Create a budget that prioritizes debt payments and limit discretionary spending.

- Seeking Professional Help: If debt becomes overwhelming, consider consulting a financial advisor or credit counseling service. They can provide guidance and support in developing a manageable plan.

- Staying Accountable: Share your debt repayment goals with a trusted friend or family member. Accountability can help keep you motivated and on track.

9.6 The Importance of Financial Education in Debt Management

Understanding the principles of personal finance is vital for effective debt management:

- Educate Yourself: Take advantage of resources such as books, online courses, and workshops to enhance your financial literacy. The more you know, the better equipped you are to make informed decisions.
- Learn About Debt Types: Familiarize yourself with the different types of debt and their implications. Understanding how interest works and the impact of late payments can help you avoid common pitfalls.
- Stay Informed About Your Rights: Knowing your rights as a borrower can empower you to advocate for yourself. Familiarize yourself with consumer protection laws and resources available to those struggling with debt.

Comprehension
Q&A

Reflect on what you've learned in this chapter by answering the following questions.

Q1 Differentiate between good debt and bad debt. Provide examples of each.

Q2 What are the impacts of debt on your financial health?

Q3 Describe effective strategies for managing debt.

Q4 How do you create a debt repayment plan, and what should it include?

Q5 Discuss the role of financial education in managing debt.

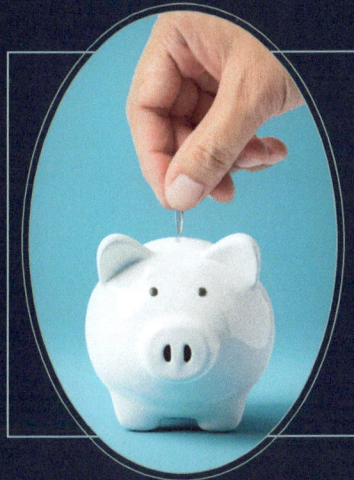

CHAPTER TEN
SAVINGS CHALLENGES

10.1 Benefits of Savings Challenges

Savings challenges can motivate individuals to save effectively and consistently. Key benefits include:

- Increased Motivation: Challenges create a sense of competition and accountability, encouraging participants to stick to their saving plans.

- Building Savings Habits: Participating in challenges fosters good saving habits by encouraging regular contributions. Over time, these habits can lead to significant savings accumulation.

- Achieving Goals: Challenges can help individuals reach specific savings goals faster. For example, a group savings challenge can encourage participants to meet a common goal, such as funding a trip or purchasing a shared experience.

Explanation: Savings challenges make saving fun and engaging, providing a structured way to build savings habits while achieving financial goals.

10.2 Types of Savings Challenges

There are various savings challenges designed to help individuals save money while making the process enjoyable:

1. 52-Week Savings Challenge: This popular challenge encourages participants to save an increasing amount each week, starting with $1 in the first week and $52 in the last week, resulting in a total of $1,378 by the end of the year. This gradual increase makes it manageable for many.

2. No-Spend Challenge: Participants commit to not spending money on non-essential items for a set period (usually a month). This challenge helps individuals reassess their spending habits and prioritize saving.

3. Save the Change Challenge: Round up purchases to the nearest dollar and save the difference. For example, if you spend $3.75 on coffee, you would save $0.25. Over time, these small amounts can add up significantly.

Explanation: Each type of savings challenge offers a unique approach to saving and can be tailored to fit individual preferences and financial situations.

10.3 Creating Your Own Savings Challenge

Designing a personalized savings challenge can be an effective way to meet your financial goals:

- Set a Target Amount: Determine how much you want to save by the end of the challenge. This could be a specific dollar amount or a percentage of your income.
- Choose a Time Frame: Decide how long the challenge will last. It could be a month, a quarter, or even a full year.
- Define Rules: Establish rules for your challenge. For instance, specify what counts as savings (e.g., only direct deposits into a savings account) and whether you'll allow exceptions for emergencies.

-Track Progress: Use a tracking sheet or app to monitor your savings throughout the challenge. Celebrate small milestones to keep motivation high.

Christmas Savings Challeng

WEEK	DEPOSIT	TOTAL
Week 1	$10	$10
Week 2	$10	$20
Week 3	$15	$35
Week 4	$15	$50
Week 5	$15	
Week 6	$15	
Week 7	$20	
Week 8	$20	
Week 9	$20	
Week 10		
Week		

Comprehension
Q&A

Reflect on what you've learned in this chapter by answering the following questions.

Q1 What are some benefits of participating in savings challenges?

Q2 Describe at least three different types of savings challenges and their objectives.

Q3 How can creating a personalized savings challenge enhance motivation and accountability?

Q4 What strategies can you implement to stay on track during a savings challenge?

Q5 Share an example of a savings challenge you would like to try and how you plan to execute it.

CHAPTER ELEVEN
INTRODUCTION TO INVESTING

11.1 What is Investing?

Investing involves allocating money to assets with the expectation of generating a return over time. It is a key component of building wealth and achieving financial goals. Unlike saving, which typically involves putting money into a low-risk account with minimal returns, investing seeks to grow your money through various assets.

Explanation: Investing is essential for long-term financial health, allowing individuals to build wealth that can outpace inflation and contribute to future financial security.

11.2 Importance of Investing

Investing is crucial for several reasons:

- Wealth Accumulation: Investing allows individuals to grow their wealth over time, providing the potential for significant returns compared to traditional savings accounts. Over the long term, investments have historically outpaced inflation, preserving purchasing power.

- Inflation Hedge: Investments, particularly in stocks and real estate, can help protect against inflation, ensuring that purchasing power is maintained over time. This is especially important as inflation can erode the value of cash savings.

- Retirement Planning: Investing is essential for building a retirement nest egg. Relying solely on savings may not be sufficient to cover expenses in retirement, making investment growth vital to ensure a comfortable retirement.

Explanation: Understanding the importance of investing is fundamental for achieving long-term financial goals and ensuring a secure financial future.

11.3 Types of Investments

1. Stocks: Ownership shares in a company that offer the potential for capital appreciation and dividends. Stocks can provide significant returns but also come with higher risks.

2. Bonds: Debt securities issued by corporations or governments that pay interest over time. Bonds are generally considered safer than stocks but typically offer lower returns.

3. Mutual Funds: Investment vehicles that pool money from multiple investors to purchase a diversified portfolio of stocks, bonds, or other assets. Mutual funds allow investors to access a diversified portfolio without having to select individual securities.

4. Real Estate: Physical property that can generate rental income and appreciate over time. Real estate investing can provide both cash flow and long-term appreciation.

5. Exchange-Traded Funds (ETFs): Investment funds that trade on stock exchanges and typically track an index, commodity, or basket of assets. ETFs offer liquidity and diversification similar to mutual funds but often with lower fees.

Explanation: Understanding the different types of investments allows individuals to build a diversified portfolio that aligns with their financial goals and risk tolerance.

11.4 Developing an Investment Strategy

Creating an investment strategy involves several key steps:
- Assess Risk Tolerance: Determine how much risk you are willing to take with your investments. Understanding your risk tolerance helps guide your investment choices and asset allocation.
- Set Investment Goals: Define your investment objectives, whether they are for retirement, purchasing a home, or funding education. Clear goals provide direction for your investment strategy.
- Diversify Investments: Spread investments across different asset classes to reduce risk. A diversified portfolio can help protect against market volatility and potential losses.
- Monitor and Rebalance: Regularly review your investment portfolio to ensure it aligns with your goals. Rebalancing involves adjusting your asset allocation based on performance and market conditions.

Explanation: A well-defined investment strategy helps individuals navigate the complexities of investing, ensuring that their portfolio aligns with their financial goals and risk tolerance.

11.5 The Power of Compound Interest

Compound interest is a critical concept in investing:

- Understanding Compounding: Compound interest is interest earned on both the initial principal and the interest that has already accrued. This creates a snowball effect, leading to exponential growth over time.

- Starting Early: The earlier you start investing, the more time your money has to grow through compounding. Even small contributions can lead to significant wealth accumulation over the long term.

Explanation: Recognizing the benefits of compound interest emphasizes the importance of starting to invest early and consistently. It illustrates how time can significantly impact investment growth.

11.6 Investment Risks

Understanding investment risks is crucial for informed decision-making:

- Market Risk: The risk that the value of investments will fluctuate due to market conditions. Economic downturns can affect the performance of stocks and real estate.

- Credit Risk: The risk that a borrower will default on a loan or bond, leading to potential losses for investors. Understanding the creditworthiness of issuers is essential for bond investors.

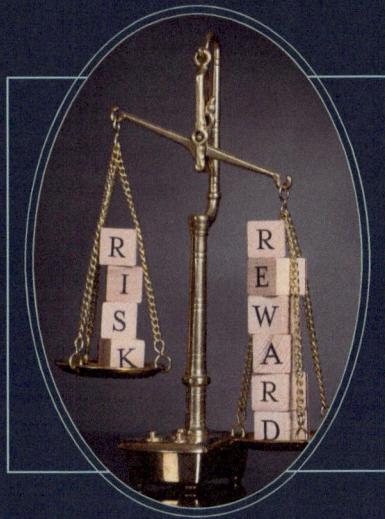

CHAPTER TWELVE
RISK VS. REWARD

12.1 Understanding Risk in Investing

Risk refers to the potential for losing money or not achieving expected returns. It is essential to evaluate risk when making investment decisions. Understanding risk helps investors make informed choices that align with their financial goals and risk tolerance.

Explanation: Recognizing the relationship between risk and reward is fundamental to effective investing. Higher potential returns often come with higher risks, and understanding this dynamic is key to successful investment strategies.

12.2 Risk Tolerance

Understanding your risk tolerance is crucial for effective investing:

- Defining Risk Tolerance: Risk tolerance is the degree of variability in investment returns that an individual is willing to withstand. Factors such as age, financial situation, and investment experience can influence risk tolerance.
- Assessing Risk Tolerance: Investors can assess their risk tolerance through questionnaires or discussions with financial advisors. This assessment can guide portfolio allocation and investment choices.

Explanation: Knowing your risk tolerance helps you build a portfolio that aligns with your comfort level and investment goals, ensuring you can withstand market fluctuations without panicking.

12.3 Evaluating Risk vs. Reward

When making investment decisions, it is critical to weigh the potential risks against the expected rewards:
- Potential Returns: Assess the potential returns of an investment and how they align with your financial goals. Higher potential returns often come with higher risks, so it is crucial to evaluate whether the potential reward justifies the risk.
- Investment Horizon: Consider how long you plan to hold an investment. Longer investment horizons may allow for greater risk-taking due to the potential for recovery from market fluctuations.

Explanation: Evaluating risk versus reward is vital for making informed investment decisions. It encourages critical thinking about potential outcomes and helps investors align their choices with their financial objectives.

12.4 Diversification as a Risk Management Strategy

Diversification is a key strategy for managing risk:

- Spreading Investments: By investing in various asset classes, industries, and geographic regions, you can reduce the impact of poor performance in any single investment.
- Balancing Risk and Reward: A diversified portfolio can help balance risk and reward, allowing you to pursue growth while minimizing potential losses.

Explanation: Diversification is one of the most effective ways to manage investment risk. It protects against market volatility and helps ensure more stable returns.

12.5 The Role of Research in Managing Risk

Conducting thorough research is vital for informed investing:

- Understanding Investments: Research potential investments to understand their fundamentals, market conditions, and historical performance. This knowledge will help you make informed decisions about where to allocate your funds.
- Staying Informed: Regularly review market trends, economic indicators, and news that may impact your investments. Staying informed can help you adjust your strategy as needed.

Explanation: Research is essential for effective risk management. It empowers investors to make informed decisions based on data and analysis rather than emotions or speculation.

12.6 The Importance of Patience in Investing

Patience is a crucial virtue in investing:

- Long-Term Perspective: Successful investing often requires a long-term perspective. Resist the urge to react to short-term market fluctuations and focus on your long-term goals.

- Avoiding Emotional Decisions: Emotional decisions can lead to impulsive actions that may harm your portfolio. Stick to your investment strategy and remain disciplined during market volatility.

Explanation: Patience in investing allows individuals to ride out market fluctuations and avoid making hasty decisions that could jeopardize long-term financial goals.

Comprehension
Q&A

Reflect on what you've learned in this chapter by answering the following questions.

Q1 What is risk in the context of investing, and why is it important to understand?

Q2 How do you evaluate risk versus reward when making investment decisions?

Q3 What is risk tolerance, and why is it important for investors?

Q4 Discuss the difference between long-term and short-term investing.

Q5 Provide an example of an investment you would consider and explain your reasoning based on risk and reward.

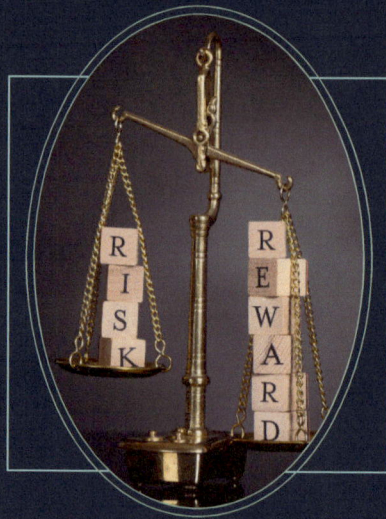

CHAPTER THIRTEEN
GROWING YOUR WEALTH THROUGH INVESTMENTS

13.1 What Is an Investment?

An investment is the act of committing money or capital to an asset, project, or venture with the expectation of generating income or profit over time. Simply put, it's putting your money to work for you.

13.2 Why Investments Matter in Personal Finance

Investing is essential for building long-term wealth, beating inflation, and achieving financial goals that saving alone may not accomplish. Whether you're preparing for retirement, buying a home, or funding your child's education, investing helps your money grow beyond what it could through a savings account.

13.3 Types of Consumer Investments

Here are some common types of investments that consumers typically explore:

- Stocks – Ownership shares in companies. High return potential but higher risk.
- Bonds – Loans to governments or corporations. Lower risk, steady income.
- Mutual Funds/ETFs – Pooled investments that spread risk across assets.
- Real Estate – Property investments that can generate rental income and appreciation.
- Retirement Accounts – Tax-advantaged accounts like 401(k)s and IRAs.
- Commodities – Physical goods like gold, oil, or agricultural products.
- Cryptocurrency – Digital assets with high volatility and risk.

13.4 How to Develop a Personal Investment Strategy

1. Set Clear Goals – Know what you're investing for (retirement, a house, etc.).
2. Assess Your Risk Tolerance – Understand how much risk you can handle emotionally and financially.
3. Choose the Right Accounts – Use accounts that match your goals, such as a Roth IRA or a taxable brokerage.
4. Start Small, Stay Consistent – Regular contributions—even small ones—can grow significantly over time.
5. Educate Yourself – The more you know, the better decisions you'll make.
6. Review and Adjust – Check your investments regularly and update them as your goals or circumstances change.

13.5 The Importance of Asset Allocation

Asset allocation is how you divide your investments among categories like stocks, bonds, and cash. It helps balance risk and reward based on your personal financial goals, time horizon, and risk tolerance. A well-diversified portfolio can minimize the impact of market fluctuations by spreading out risk.

13.6 Example: Setting a Short-Term Investment Goal

- Goal: Save for a home down payment in 5 years
- Target Amount: $40,000
- Monthly Contribution: $650/month
- Suggested Allocation: 60% in conservative growth stocks, 40% in bonds

Review Plan: Annually, adjusting contributions or allocations if needed

Comprehension
Q&A

Reflect on what you've learned in this chapter by answering the following questions.

Q1 Define investing and explain its signifigance in personal finance.

Q2 What are the different types of investments available to consumers?

Q3 How can you develop a personal investment strategy?

Q4 Discuss the importance of asset allocation in managing investment risks.

Q5 Provide an example of an investment goal you would like to acheive.

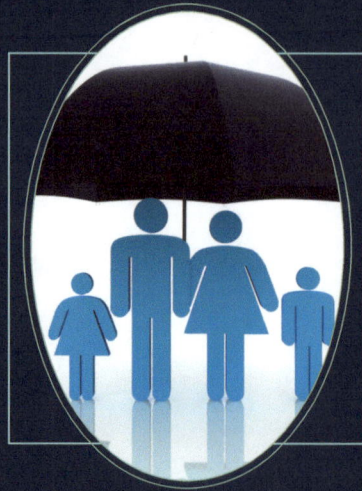

CHAPTER FOURTEEN
INSURANCE BASICS

14.1 What is Insurance?

Insurance is a financial product that provides protection against financial loss. It is an essential component of a sound financial strategy, helping individuals manage risk and protect their assets. Insurance helps mitigate the financial impact of unexpected events, such as accidents, illnesses, or property damage. It operates on the principle of risk-sharing, where individuals or businesses pay premiums into a pool managed by an insurance provider. In return, the insurer provides financial coverage or compensation for specified losses or damages as outlined in the policy. This arrangement ensures that the financial burden of significant, unforeseen events is distributed across many contributors, offering policyholders peace of mind and financial stability when faced with unexpected challenges.

Explanation: Understanding insurance is crucial for effective risk management. It allows individuals to safeguard their financial future and ensure they have the resources to recover from an emergency.

14.2 Types of Insurance

1. Health Insurance: Covers medical expenses and healthcare costs, helping individuals access necessary medical care without incurring significant financial burdens. Understanding your health insurance plan, including premiums, deductibles, and coverage limits, is crucial for effective healthcare management.

2. Auto Insurance: Provides coverage for vehicles and liability in case of accidents. Auto insurance typically includes various types of coverage, such as liability, collision, and comprehensive insurance, allowing drivers to protect themselves and their vehicles.

3. Homeowners Insurance: Protects property and belongings against damage or theft. Homeowners insurance can cover various risks, including fire, theft, and natural disasters. Understanding policy specifics, such as coverage limits and deductibles, is essential for adequate protection.

4. Life Insurance: Provides financial support to beneficiaries in the event of the policyholder's death. Life insurance can be term-based or whole life, each with different features and benefits. Evaluating your life insurance needs based on your family's financial situation is crucial.

Explanation: Understanding the different types of insurance allows individuals to choose the right coverage for their needs. Each type serves a specific purpose and provides essential protection.

14.3 The Importance of Insurance

Insurance is important for several reasons:

- Risk Management: Insurance can protect against significant financial losses due to unforeseen events, such as accidents or medical emergencies. Having the right insurance coverage can provide peace of mind and help prevent financial hardship.

- Peace of Mind: Having insurance coverage provides reassurance, knowing that you have a safety net in place. This reassurance allows individuals to focus on other aspects of their lives without the constant worry of potential financial loss.
- Financial Planning: Insurance plays a crucial role in overall financial planning, ensuring that unexpected events do not derail your financial goals. Integrating insurance into your financial strategy can help protect your assets and ensure long-term stability.

Explanation: The importance of insurance cannot be overstated. It provides individuals with a sense of security and helps mitigate the financial risks associated with everyday life.

14.4 Evaluating Insurance Needs

Assessing your insurance needs involves several steps:

1. Identify Risks: Consider the potential risks you face, such as health issues, accidents, or property damage. Understanding these risks can help you determine the necessary coverage.
2. Determine Coverage Amounts: Evaluate how much coverage you need for each type of insurance based on your financial situation and responsibilities. For example, consider factors such as income, debts, and dependents when determining life insurance needs.
3. Review Policies Regularly: Regularly review your insurance policies to ensure they still meet your needs. Life changes, such as marriage or the birth of a child, may require adjustments to your coverage.

Explanation: Evaluating insurance needs is a proactive approach to risk management. Regular assessments ensure that coverage remains relevant and adequate for changing life circumstances.

Explanation: Keeping track of your insurance coverage helps ensure you have adequate protection. Regular reviews can identify gaps in coverage or opportunities to adjust policies based on changing needs.

Tips for Evaluation of Policies:

- *Compare Premium Costs: Ensure you're getting the best value for coverage provided.*
- *Check Deductibles: Make sure they're affordable in case of a claim.*
- *Understand Renewal Terms: Note the renewal date and any changes to premiums.*
- *Evaluate Coverage: Confirm the policy meets your specific needs (e.g., family size, assets).*
- *Research Provider Reputation: Look for reviews or ratings of the insurer.*

See the checklist on the following page that outlines all the various types of insurance you should consider to ensure you have proper coverage.

CHECKLIST & TIPS FOR
Insurance Coverage

☑ **Health Insurance**
- Provider: ABC Insurance
- Coverage Amount: $500,000
- Premium Cost: $300/month
- Renewal Date: 06/01/2024
- Notes: Check for copays and network restrictions.

☑ **Auto Insurance**
- Provider: XYZ Insurance
- Coverage Amount: $100,000
- Premium Cost: $100/month
- Renewal Date: 05/15/2024
- Notes: Ensure full coverage, including collision and liability.

☑ **Homeowners Insurance**
- Provider: QRS Insurance
- Coverage Amount: $250,000
- Premium Cost: $150/month
- Renewal Date: 04/01/2024
- Notes: Review deductibles and coverage for natural disasters.

☑ **Life Insurance**
- Provider: LMN Insurance
- Coverage Amount: $300,000
- Premium Cost: $50/month
- Renewal Date: 02/01/2024
- Notes: Assess beneficiary needs and policy terms.

Comprehension
Q&A

Reflect on what you've learned in this chapter by answering the following questions.

Q1   Define insurance and explain its importance in personal finance.

Q2   List and describe different types of insurance policies individuals should consider.

Q3   How often should you evaluate your insurance coverage?

Q4   What factors should you consider when selecting an insurance provider?

Q5   Explain the difference between premiums and deductibles.

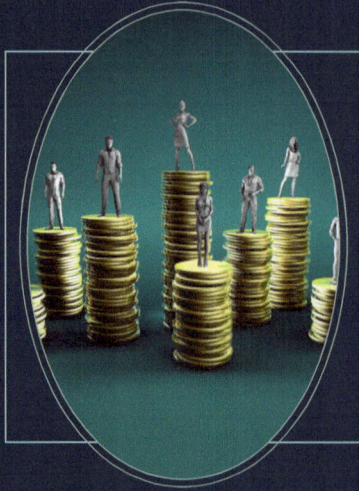

CHAPTER FIFTHTEEN

CREATING AN INVESTMENT PLAN

15.1 Importance of an Investment Plan

An investment plan provides a roadmap for your investment journey. It helps you align your investments with your financial goals, ensuring that your strategy is tailored to your specific needs and circumstances. A well-defined investment plan can also help you remain focused and disciplined in your investment approach.

Explanation: Having a clear investment plan is crucial for successful investing. It helps individuals navigate market fluctuations and stay committed to their long-term financial goals.

15.2 Setting Investment Goals

Setting clear investment goals is essential for effective investing:

- Define Your Objectives: Identify what you want to achieve with your investments. Common objectives include retirement savings, funding education, or purchasing a home.
- Time Horizon: Determine how long you plan to invest before needing the funds. Understanding your time horizon can help guide your asset allocation decisions.
- Specificity: Make your goals specific and measurable. For example, instead of saying, "I want to save for retirement," a specific goal could be, "I want to accumulate $500,000 in my retirement account by age 65."

Explanation: Setting investment goals provides direction for your investment strategy. Specific goals help you measure progress and adjust your plan as necessary.

15.3 Developing an Investment Strategy

Creating a well-thought-out investment strategy involves several key steps:

1. Assess Risk Tolerance: Determine how much risk you are willing to take with your investments. Understanding your risk tolerance helps guide your investment choices.
2. Diversification: Spread investments across different asset classes to mitigate risk. A diversified portfolio can help protect against market volatility and potential losses.
3. Choose Investment Vehicles: Decide which types of investments align with your goals and risk tolerance. This could include stocks, bonds, mutual funds, or real estate.
4. Monitor and Rebalance: Regularly review your investment portfolio to ensure it aligns with your goals. Rebalancing involves adjusting your asset allocation based on performance and market conditions.

Explanation: A comprehensive investment strategy helps individuals make informed decisions and adapt their portfolios to changing market conditions and personal circumstances.

Sample Investment Plan Outline

Retirement Savings

- Asset Allocation: 60% Stocks, 30% Bonds, 10% Real Estate
- Target Amount: $1,000,000
- Time Horizon: 30 years
- Notes: Reassess allocation every 5 years to adjust for risk tolerance and market conditions.

Education Savings

- Asset Allocation: 70% Stocks, 30% Bonds
- Target Amount: $100,000
- Time Horizon: 15 years
- Notes: Use a 529 plan to maximize tax benefits and focus on stable growth as the time horizon shortens.

Emergency Fund

- Asset Allocation: 100% High-Yield Savings or Money Market Fund
- Target Amount: 6 months of living expenses (~$30,000)
- Time Horizon: Ongoing
- Notes: Ensure quick liquidity and low risk; review annually for adequacy.

Short-Term Goals (e.g., House Down Payment)

- Asset Allocation: 40% Bonds, 40% Money Market, 20% Stocks
- Target Amount: $50,000
- Time Horizon: 5 years
- Notes: Prioritize low-risk investments to preserve capital.

Wealth Building

- Asset Allocation: 80% Stocks, 10% Bonds, 10% Alternative Investments (e.g., REITs, Commodities)
- Target Amount: Flexible
- Time Horizon: 20+ years
- Notes: Focus on high-growth assets and rebalance annually.

Checklist Tips for Customizing Your Investment Plan

1. Set Clear Goals: Define specific amounts and time frames for each goal.
2. Diversify: Spread investments across different asset classes to manage risk.
3. Review Regularly: Assess progress and adjust allocations annually or during life changes.
4. Risk Assessment: Align your asset allocation with your risk tolerance and time horizon.
5. Tax Efficiency: Use tax-advantaged accounts like IRAs, 529 plans, or HSAs.

15.4 Monitoring and Rebalancing Your Portfolio

Regularly monitoring your investment portfolio is critical for staying aligned with your goals:

- Performance Review: Schedule periodic reviews to assess how your investments are performing. This can help you identify underperforming assets and make necessary adjustments.
- Rebalancing: If certain investments grow significantly, they may *take up a larger portion of your portfolio than intended. Rebalance by selling some of those investments and reallocating to underrepresented areas to maintain your desired asset allocation.*

Explanation: Monitoring and rebalancing your portfolio is essential for maintaining risk levels and ensuring that your investments align with your long-term objectives.

15.5 The Role of Professional Advisors

Consider the benefits of consulting with financial advisors:

- Expertise: Financial advisors can provide professional guidance tailored to your specific financial situation and goals. They can help you navigate complex financial decisions and develop a customized investment strategy.
- Investment Management: Advisors can manage your investment portfolio, relieving you of the day-to-day responsibilities of monitoring and making investment decisions. This can be particularly beneficial for individuals with limited time or expertise in investing.

Explanation: Engaging with financial advisors can enhance your investment strategy and provide reassurance that your portfolio is being managed effectively.

Comprehension
Q&A

Reflect on what you've learned in this chapter by answering the following questions.

Q1   Why is it important to set clear investment goals?

Q2   Describe the key components of a well-developed investment strategy.

Q3   How does risk tolerance influence investment decisions?

Q4   Discuss the purpose of rebalancing an investment portfolio.

Q5   When should you consider seeking professional financial advice?

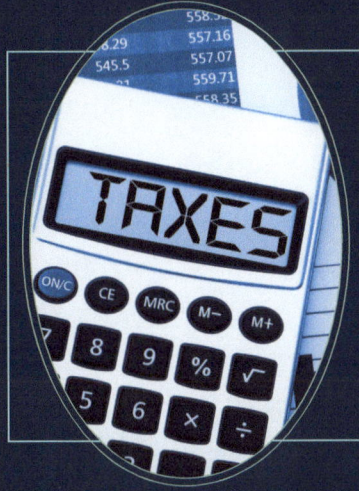

CHAPTER SIXTEEN
TAXES

16.1 Understanding Taxes

Taxes are mandatory financial charges imposed by governments. Understanding taxes is crucial for effective financial planning and maximizing savings. Taxes can take various forms, including income tax, capital gains tax, and property tax.

Explanation: Familiarity with tax obligations helps individuals manage their finances more effectively. It can lead to better financial decision-making and optimization of tax liabilities.

16.2 Types of Taxes

1. Income Tax: Tax on earnings from employment, investments, and other sources of income. Income tax is typically progressive, meaning that higher income levels are taxed at higher rates.

2. Capital Gains Tax: Tax on profits from the sale of assets or investments. The rate may differ based on whether the asset was held long-term or short-term.

3. Property Tax: Tax based on the value of owned real estate, usually levied by local governments. Property taxes contribute to funding local services, such as schools and public safety.

4. Sales Tax: Tax imposed on the sale of goods and services, typically collected at the point of sale. Sales tax rates vary by state and locality.

Explanation: Understanding the different types of taxes allows individuals to prepare for their tax liabilities effectively. It helps in making informed financial decisions throughout the year.

16.3 Tax Brackets and Rates

Familiarize yourself with tax brackets and how they apply to your income:

- Progressive Tax System: In many countries, tax rates increase as income rises. Understanding how your income fits into tax brackets can help you estimate your tax liability.

- Tax Credits and Deductions: Tax credits reduce the amount of tax owed, while deductions reduce taxable income. Knowing available credits and deductions can significantly impact your tax bill.

Explanation: Awareness of tax brackets and available credits/deductions can lead to effective tax planning, helping individuals minimize their overall tax burden.

16.4 Tax Planning Strategies

Implementing tax planning strategies can maximize your savings:

- Retirement Contributions: Contributing to retirement accounts like 401(k)s or IRAs can lower your taxable income while saving for the future. This strategy not only aids in retirement planning but also reduces your current tax liability.
- Tax Loss Harvesting: Selling investments that have lost value to offset gains from profitable investments can reduce your tax liability. This strategy helps to minimize the impact of capital gains taxes.

Explanation: Tax planning is an ongoing process that involves proactive measures to optimize tax liabilities. It allows individuals to keep more of their income and grow their wealth.

16.5 Keeping Track of Tax Documents

Organizing tax documents is essential for efficient tax filing:
- Maintain Records: Keep records of income, expenses, and deductions throughout the year. Use digital tools or apps to track receipts and invoices.
- Prepare for Tax Season: As tax season approaches, gather necessary documents, such as W-2s, 1099s, and receipts for deductible expenses.

Explanation: Maintaining organized records simplifies the tax filing process, reduces the likelihood of errors, and ensures that individuals take full advantage of available deductions and credits.

Checklist Tips for Tracking Tax Deductions and Credits

- Organize Documents: Keep receipts, forms, and statements in one place for tax preparation.

- Understand Limits: Know the income or contribution limits for each deduction or credit.

- Use Tax Software or a CPA: To ensure accurate filing and maximize eligible deductions.

- Review Updates: Tax laws can change annually, so check for any new or expiring credits.

TAX DEEDUCTIONS & CREDITS TRACKER

Mortgage Interest
- Amount:_____
- Eligibility Criteria: Primary residence only.
- Notes: Must itemize deductions to claim; retain Form 1098 from your lender.

Charitable Donations
- Amount: _____
- Eligibility Criteria: Contributions must be to qualified organizations.
- Notes: Keep all receipts or acknowledgments; ensure documentation for donations over $250.

Child Tax Credit
- Amount: *Standard is $2,000 per child (Check Currrent Tax Law)* Your Amount:_____
- Eligibility Criteria: Dependent must be under 17 years old and meet IRS requirements.
- Notes: Verify adjusted gross income (AGI) limits for full credit eligibility.

Education Expenses (Lifetime Learning Credit)
- Amount: Up to $2,000
- Eligibility Criteria: Qualified tuition and fees for higher education.
- Notes: Check for income phase-out thresholds; Form 1098-T required.

Medical Expenses
- Amount: Varies
- Eligibility Criteria: Expenses must exceed 7.5% of AGI.
- Notes: Keep detailed records and receipts for all eligible expenses.
- Amount: _____

State and Local Taxes (SALT)
- Amount: Up to $10,000 | Your Amount: _____
- Eligibility Criteria: Includes property, income, or sales taxes.
- Notes: Deduction limit applies; consider impact on itemizing.

Retirement Savings Contributions Credit (Saver's Credit)
- Amount: Up to $1,000 (single) or $2,000 (married filing jointly)
- Eligibility Criteria: Income below specified thresholds; contribute to IRA or 401(k).
- Notes: Check eligibility limits based on filing status and income.
- Your Amount:_____

Comprehension
Q&A

Reflect on what you've learned in this chapter by answering the following questions.

Q1 What are the different types of taxes individuals may encounter?

Q2 Explain the difference between tax credits and tax deductions.

Q3 How can tax planning strategies help minimize tax liability?

Q4 Why is it important to keep organized records for tax purposes?

Q5 Discuss the significance of understanding tax brackets and rates in personal finance.

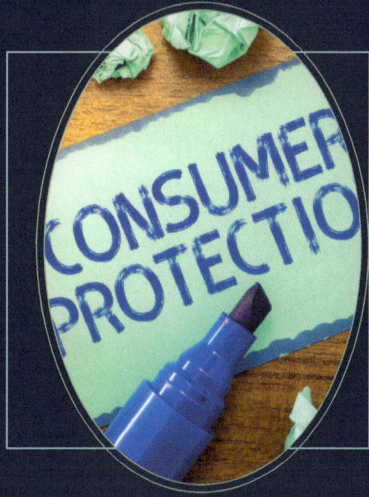

CHAPTER SEVENTEEN
CONSUMER RIGHTS AND RESPONSIBILITIES

17.1 Understanding Consumer Rights

Consumers have rights that protect them in transactions involving goods and services. Familiarizing yourself with these rights can empower you as a consumer and ensure you make informed decisions when purchasing products or services.

Explanation: Understanding consumer rights is essential for navigating the marketplace effectively. It helps individuals advocate for themselves and ensures they receive fair treatment.

17.2 Key Consumer Rights

1. Right to Information: Consumers have the right to receive clear and accurate information about products and services, enabling them to make informed decisions. This includes details about ingredients, pricing, and warranties.

2. Right to Safety: Consumers are entitled to safe products that do not pose a risk to health or safety. This right protects individuals from harmful or defective products.

3. Right to Redress: Consumers have the right to seek compensation for unsatisfactory or defective products or services. This right enables consumers to file complaints and receive refunds or replacements.

4. Right to Choose: Consumers have the right to select from a variety of goods and services in the marketplace, promoting competition and fair pricing.

Explanation: Knowing and advocating for consumer rights enhances confidence in making purchasing decisions. It ensures that consumers are treated fairly and can seek resolution when issues arise.

17.3 Responsibilities of Consumers

Along with rights, consumers also have responsibilities:

- Informed Decision-Making: Consumers should research products and services before making purchases, which includes reading product reviews and comparing prices.

- Reporting Issues: If encountering problems with products or services, consumers should report issues to the appropriate authorities. This could involve filing complaints with consumer protection agencies or contacting the retailer directly.

- Respecting Terms and Conditions: Consumers should understand and adhere to the terms and conditions of purchases, including warranties and return policies. This ensures a smoother transaction and helps avoid misunderstandings.

Explanation: Being a responsible consumer entails being informed and proactive. Consumers should take ownership of their purchasing decisions and advocate for themselves when necessary.

17.4 Protecting Yourself as a Consumer

Here are some strategies to protect yourself while shopping:

- Read Reviews: Research products and read reviews from other consumers to ensure quality and reliability. Online reviews can provide valuable insights into product performance and customer satisfaction.

- Use Secure Payment Methods: Utilize secure payment methods, such as credit cards, to protect against fraud and unauthorized transactions. Credit cards often offer additional protections against fraud and disputes.

- Know Return Policies: Familiarize yourself with the return policies of retailers to avoid surprises if you need to return or exchange an item. Knowing the return window and requirements can save time and effort.

Explanation: Protecting yourself as a consumer involves being informed and cautious. Taking the necessary steps can help individuals avoid scams or unsatisfactory purchases.

CONSUMER RIGHTS

Right to Information

Right to Safety

Right to Redress

Right to Choose

CHECKLIST

For Protecting Your Consumer Rights

☑ **Right to Information**
- Description: Accurate information about products.
- Action Steps:
  - Always read labels, user manuals, and reviews.
  - Ask questions to clarify product details.

☑ **Right to Safety**
- Description: Safe and hazard-free products.
- Action Steps:
  - Check safety certifications and standards.
  - Report unsafe products to the relevant authorities or consumer agencies.

☑ **Right to Redress**
- Description: Compensation for defective or substandard products.
- Action Steps:
  - Keep purchase receipts and warranty documents.
  - Document defects with photos or videos.
  - File a formal complaint with the seller or manufacturer.

☑ **Right to Choose**
- Description: Access to a variety of goods and services.
- Action Steps:
  - Compare products and services before making a decision.
  - Avoid monopolized markets or restrictive options.

Comprehension
Q&A

Reflect on what you've learned in this chapter by answering the following questions.

01 What are the key consumer rights that protect individuals in transactions?

02 Describe the responsibilities consumers have in addition to their rights.

03 Why is it important for consumers to be informed about their rights?

04 Discuss strategies consumers can use to protect themselves while shopping.

05 Provide an example of a consumer issue you or someone you know has faced and how it was resolved.

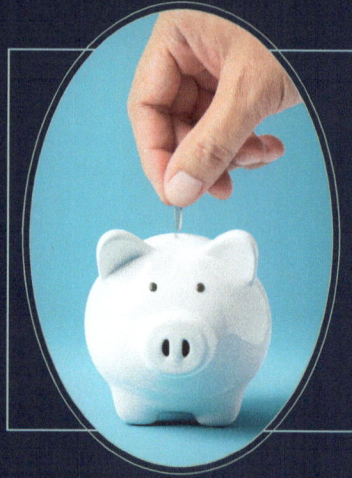

CHAPTER EIGHTEEN
INVESTING IN REAL ESTATE

18.1 Understanding Real Estate Investment

Investing in real estate offers various strategies beyond direct property ownership. Options such as Real Estate Investment Trusts (REITs) allow individuals to invest in real estate portfolios without managing physical properties, providing diversification and liquidity. Additionally, platforms facilitating real estate crowdfunding enable investors to participate in property ventures with lower capital requirements, broadening access to the real estate market. Each investment approach carries its own set of risks and rewards. It's essential to conduct thorough due diligence, understand market dynamics, and assess personal financial goals before committing to a particular real estate investment strategy.

Explanation: Real estate investing can diversify an investment portfolio and provide additional income sources. Understanding the nuances of real estate can lead to significant financial rewards.

18.2 Types of Real Estate Investments

1. Residential Properties: Investing in single-family homes, condominiums, or multi-family units for rental income. This type of investment can provide a steady cash flow and potential appreciation in property value.

2. Commercial Properties: Purchasing office buildings, retail spaces, or warehouses that generate income through leases. Commercial properties typically require a larger investment but can yield higher returns compared to residential properties.

3. Real Estate Investment Trusts (REITs): Investing in publicly traded companies that own, operate, or finance income-generating real estate. REITs offer investors a way to invest in real estate without directly purchasing properties, providing diversification and liquidity.

4. Raw Land: Purchasing undeveloped land with the potential for future development or resale. Raw land can appreciate significantly over time, especially in growing areas.

Explanation: Each type of real estate investment has unique characteristics, risks, and benefits. Understanding these differences allows investors to make informed decisions based on their financial goals.

18.3 Benefits of Real Estate Investing

- Cash Flow: Rental properties can provide a steady stream of income, contributing to financial security. Positive cash flow allows investors to reinvest profits and grow their portfolio.

- Appreciation: Real estate often appreciates over time, allowing investors to profit from increased property values when sold. Understanding market trends is essential for maximizing appreciation potential.

- Tax Advantages: Real estate investors can benefit from tax deductions, such as mortgage interest, property taxes, depreciation, and certain expenses related to property management. These deductions can significantly reduce taxable income, enhancing overall profitability.

Explanation: The benefits of real estate investing can lead to significant financial growth and security. Understanding these advantages can motivate individuals to explore real estate as an investment option.

18.4 Risks of Real Estate Investing

While real estate can be a lucrative investment, it also comes with risks that investors must consider:

- Market Fluctuations: Real estate markets can be volatile, and property values may decline during economic downturns. Investors should stay informed about market trends and be prepared for fluctuations.
- Management Responsibilities: Owning rental properties involves managing tenants, maintenance, and repairs, which can be time-consuming. Investors must be prepared to handle tenant issues, property upkeep, and emergency repairs.
- Illiquidity: Real estate is less liquid than stocks or bonds, as selling a property can take time and incur costs. Investors should be aware of the potential challenges of accessing cash from real estate investments.

Explanation: Understanding the risks associated with real estate investing is essential for making informed decisions. Being aware of potential challenges can help investors prepare and mitigate risks effectively.

18.5 Steps to Start Investing in Real Estate

Investing in real estate requires careful planning and research. Here are essential steps to get started:

1. Research the Market: Understand local real estate trends, property values, and rental rates. Explore different neighborhoods to identify areas with growth potential.

2. Determine Your Budget: Establish a clear budget for purchasing a property, including down payment, closing costs, and ongoing expenses. It's crucial to have a realistic understanding of your financial capabilities.

3. Explore Financing Options: Investigate various financing options, such as traditional mortgages, FHA loans, or private lenders. Understanding the terms and conditions of each option is essential for finding the best fit for your situation.

4. Conduct Due Diligence: Thoroughly inspect potential properties and evaluate their condition, location, and appreciation potential. This includes reviewing property history, zoning regulations, and any potential issues that may arise.

5. Make an Offer: Once you've found a suitable property, make a competitive offer based on your research and analysis. Be prepared to negotiate and consider contingencies such as inspections and appraisals.

Explanation: Taking a systematic approach to real estate investing can help individuals make informed decisions and minimize risks. Thorough research and preparation are essential for success.

Real Estate Investment Budget Template

Category	Estimated Cost	Actual Cost	Notes
Purchase Price			Include negotiated purchase price.
Closing Costs			Include attorney fees, title insurance, etc.
Repair Costs			Estimate based on inspection and contractor quotes.
Monthly Mortgage Payment			Include principal, interest, and PMI if applicable.
Property Management Fees			Applicable for rental properties; typically 8-12% of rent.
Insurance			Homeowners or landlord insurance premiums.
Property Taxes			Verify annual property taxes based on local rates.
Miscellaneous Costs			Budget for utilities, HOA fees, or unexpected expenses.
Total			Sum of all categories above.

Checklist for Using the Template

- **Estimate Costs:**

Use recent quotes, inspection reports, and local data to provide accurate estimates for each category.

- **Track Actual Costs:**

Update with actual expenses during the purchase and renovation phases.

- **Take Notes:**

Add any relevant details (e.g., unexpected expenses, adjustments made, or cost overruns).

- **Calculate Total:**

Regularly update the total for accurate budget tracking.

- **Review Regularly:**

Compare actual costs to estimates to adjust future projections and investment strategies.

Pro Tips for Success

Do Due Diligence: Conduct thorough market research to avoid underestimating costs.

Account for Reserves: Set aside 10-20% of the total cost for unexpected repairs or vacancies.

Analyze ROI: Use the updated budget to calculate cash flow, cap rate, and return on investment.

Comprehension
Q&A

Reflect on what you've learned in this chapter by answering the following questions.

Q1   What are the benefits of investing in real estate?

Q2   Describe the different types of real estate investments and provide examples of each.

Q3   What steps should you take before investing in real estate?

Q4   Discuss the risks associated with real estate investing.

Q5   How can you determine the potential profitability of a real estate investment?

CHAPTER NINETEEN
BUILDING WEALTH THROUGH ENTREPRENEURSHIP

19.1 Understanding Entrepreneurship

Entrepreneurship involves starting and running a business to create value and generate profit. It can be a path to financial independence and wealth building. Entrepreneurs often identify gaps in the market and develop innovative solutions to meet consumer needs, creating opportunities for themselves and others.

Explanation: Entrepreneurship offers a unique avenue for wealth creation. It allows individuals to leverage their skills and passions to build businesses that can generate income and create jobs.

19.2 Benefits of Entrepreneurship

- Financial Freedom: Successful entrepreneurs can achieve financial independence by creating multiple income streams. Owning a business allows for greater control over income potential compared to traditional employment.

- Flexibility: Entrepreneurship allows for greater control over your schedule and work-life balance. Entrepreneurs can design their work environment and set their own hours, leading to a more fulfilling lifestyle.
- Personal Fulfillment: Entrepreneurs often pursue their passions, leading to greater job satisfaction and fulfillment. Building a business around a personal interest can create a deep sense of purpose and motivation.

Explanation: The benefits of entrepreneurship extend beyond financial rewards. They include personal growth, flexibility, and the opportunity to make a positive impact on society.

19.3 Types of Business Models

1. Service-Based Businesses: Offering services to clients, such as consulting, coaching, or freelance work. These businesses often require low startup costs and can scale based on demand.
2. Product-Based Businesses: Selling physical or digital products through retail, e-commerce, or direct sales. This model may involve more upfront investment for inventory and production.
3. Franchising: Operating a business under an established brand name, benefiting from the parent company's support and resources. Franchising can reduce risks associated with starting a new business by leveraging an existing brand.

Explanation: Understanding the various business models allows aspiring entrepreneurs to choose the one that aligns best with their skills, resources, and market opportunities.

19.4 Steps to Starting a Business

1. Identify Your Niche: Research the market to find a unique product or service that meets consumer needs. Understanding your target audience is crucial for market entry.

2. Create a Business Plan: Outline your business goals, target market, marketing strategies, and financial projections. A well-structured business plan serves as a roadmap for your entrepreneurial journey.

3. Secure Financing: Explore funding options, such as personal savings, bank loans, or investors. Understanding your financing needs will help you determine the best approach for your startup.

4. Register Your Business: Choose a legal structure for your business (e.g., LLC, corporation) and register it with the appropriate authorities. Ensure compliance with local laws and regulations.

5. Launch Your Business: Implement your marketing strategies and officially open for business. Use digital marketing, social media, and networking to attract customers.

Explanation: Starting a business involves careful planning and execution. Each step is critical to establishing a successful venture that can thrive in the marketplace.

Business Startup Budget Template

Category	Estimated Cost	Actual Cost	Notes
Equipment			Include tools, machinery, technology, etc.
Inventory			Stock needed to launch operations.
Marketing Expenses			Costs for advertising, branding, and promotions.
Office Supplies			Stationery, furniture, and other essentials.
Website Development			Design, hosting, domain registration, etc.
Legal and Licensing Fees			Fees for business registration, permits, and contracts.
Miscellaneous Costs			Budget for unforeseen or additional expenses.
Total			Sum of all categories above.

CHECKLIST & TIPS FOR
Using the Business Startup Template

1. ☑ **Estimate Costs:**
   - Gather quotes and conduct research for each category to determine realistic estimates.
2. ☑ **Track Actual Costs:**
   - Update the template with real expenses as they are incurred during the startup process.
3. ☑ **Add Notes:**
   - Document any details or justifications for costs, such as suppliers, vendors, or unexpected adjustments.
4. ☑ **Calculate Total:**
   - Sum up all expenses regularly to ensure alignment with your budget.
5. ☑ **Reassess Periodically:**
   - Review and compare estimates vs. actual costs to make informed decisions for scaling or cutting expenses.

Pro Tips for Success

- Set Priorities: Focus on essential items that directly impact your business launch.
- Account for Contingencies: Add 10-20% of the total estimated cost as a buffer for unforeseen expenses.
- Track Cash Flow: Use this budget to evaluate whether your startup needs additional funding.
- Research Funding Options: Consider grants, loans, or investors to cover startup costs.

Comprehension
Q&A

Reflect on what you've learned in this chapter by answering the following questions.

Q1 What is entrepreneurship, and why is it important for building wealth?

Q2 List and describe the different types of business models.

Q3 What steps should you take to start a business?

Q4 Discuss the benefits and challenges of being an entrepreneur.

Q5 Provide an example of a successful entrepreneurial venture and analyze its key factors for success.

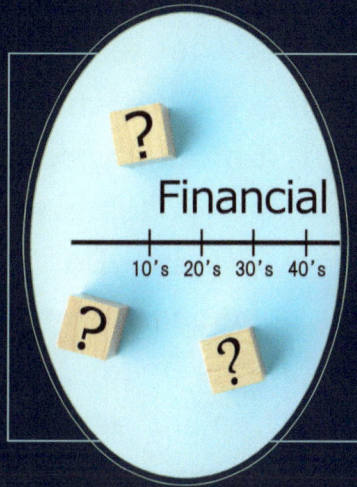

CHAPTER TWENTY

FINANCIAL PLANNING FOR LIFE EVENTS

20.1 Understanding Life Events

Life events, such as marriage, having children, buying a home, or retirement, can significantly impact your financial situation. Effective financial planning can help navigate these transitions successfully and ensure that financial goals are met despite life changes.

Explanation: Life events often require adjustments to financial plans. Proactive financial planning helps individuals adapt to changes and remain focused on long-term goals.

20.2 Financial Planning for Specific Life Events

1. Marriage: Combine finances, create a joint budget, and discuss financial goals as a couple. Open communication about money can strengthen relationships and ensure both partners are on the same page.

2. Having Children: Plan for increased expenses related to childcare, education, and healthcare. Consider setting up a savings account for future education costs, such as a 529 plan, to maximize tax benefits.

3. Buying a Home: Save for a down payment, understand mortgage options, and budget for ongoing homeownership costs, such as maintenance and property taxes. Do thorough research on neighborhoods and market conditions before making a purchase.

4. Retirement: Establish a retirement savings plan, considering factors such as desired retirement age, lifestyle, and healthcare costs. Regularly contribute to retirement accounts and review your investments to ensure alignment with your goals.

Explanation: Tailoring financial plans to specific life events ensures that individuals are prepared for the financial implications of these changes. Proactive planning helps ease transitions and minimize stress.

20.3 Creating a Financial Plan for Life Events

1. Identify Key Events: List significant life events you anticipate and their potential financial impacts. Identifying these events allows for proactive planning and preparation.

2. Set Financial Goals: Establish clear financial goals associated with each life event. For example, if expecting a child, your goal might be to save $10,000 for a child's education within 10 years.

3. Develop Action Steps: Create actionable steps to achieve your goals, including budgeting, saving, and investing. Break down larger goals into smaller, manageable steps to maintain motivation.

4. Review and Adjust: Regularly review your financial plan to ensure it aligns with your changing circumstances and goals. Life events may require adjustments to your budget and savings strategies.

Explanation: Creating a financial plan for life events provides structure and clarity, helping individuals navigate changes with confidence. Regular reviews ensure the plan remains relevant and effective.

Life Event Financial Planning Worksheet

	Life Event	Anticipated Date	Financial Goals	Action Steps
1	Marriage		Joint savings for a home	Create joint budget, open joint account
2	Having Children		Save for education	Set up 529 plan, budget for childcare
3	Buying a Home		Save $20,000 for down payment	Open dedicated savings account
4	Retirement		Accumulate $1 million	Increase retirement contributions

Top Tips for Planning for Life Events:

- Set Clear Financial Goals
- Identify the specific financial outcomes you want for each life event (e.g., saving for a wedding, buying a home, or funding education).
- Break down these goals into achievable milestones, such as saving a certain amount monthly.
- Use tools like savings calculators or budgeting apps to stay on track.
- Create a Realistic Budget
- Review your current income, expenses, and savings to allocate resources effectively.
- Prioritize expenses directly tied to the life event and cut back on non-essential spending if needed.
- Set up separate accounts for big goals to avoid dipping into those funds for other purposes.
- Plan for the Unexpected
- Build an emergency fund with at least 3-6 months of living expenses to cover unforeseen challenges during the process (e.g., medical expenses, job loss).
- Factor in potential extra costs, like unexpected fees or price increases, and add a buffer (typically 10-20% of your budget).
- Stay flexible and review your plan regularly to adjust for changes in circumstances or priorities.

Comprehension
Q&A

Reflect on what you've learned in this chapter by answering the following questions.

Q1 What are life events, and why is financial planning important during these transitions?

Q2 Describe how financial planning differs for marriage, having children, buying a home, and retirement.

Q3 Outline the steps involved in creating a financial plan for an anticipated life event.

Q4 Discuss the significance of insurance in financial planning for life events.

Q5 Provide an example of a life event you anticipate experiencing and outline your financial planning approach.

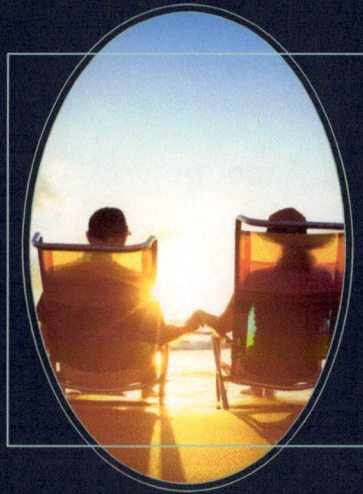

CHAPTER TWENTY-ONE
RETIREMENT PLANNING

21.1 The Importance of Retirement Planning

Planning for retirement ensures financial security in later years. It involves understanding how much money you need and how to accumulate it. Effective retirement planning requires a thorough assessment of your current finances, expenses, and retirement goals.

Explanation: Retirement planning is essential for ensuring that individuals can maintain their desired lifestyle in retirement. It involves proactive measures to secure financial stability during one of life's most significant transitions.

21.2 Setting Retirement Goals

1. Determine Retirement Age: Decide at what age you want to retire. This decision can significantly impact the amount you need to save and invest before retirement.

Explanation: Setting clear retirement goals provides a roadmap for financial planning. It allows individuals to create a targeted savings strategy that aligns with their desired retirement lifestyle.

21.3 Types of Retirement Accounts

1. 401(k) Plans: Employer-sponsored retirement plans that allow employees to save for retirement with tax advantages. Many employers offer matching contributions, which can significantly enhance your savings.

2. IRAs (Individual Retirement Accounts): Personal retirement accounts that offer tax benefits for contributions and withdrawals. Traditional IRAs allow for tax-deferred growth, while Roth IRAs provide tax-free withdrawals in retirement.

3. Roth IRAs: A type of IRA where contributions are made with after-tax dollars, allowing for tax-free withdrawals in retirement. This can be advantageous for individuals who expect to be in a higher tax bracket during retirement.

Explanation: Understanding the different types of retirement accounts is crucial for effective retirement planning. Each account has unique features, benefits, and tax implications that can impact long-term savings.

21.4 The Power of Compound Interest in Retirement Savings

Compound interest is a critical factor in retirement savings:

- Understanding Compounding: The earlier you start saving for retirement, the more your money can grow through compounding. Even small contributions can lead to significant growth over time.
- Starting Early: Investing early in retirement accounts can yield substantial benefits. For instance, contributing $200 monthly to a retirement account at a 7% return over 30 years can result in over $200,000 in savings.

Explanation: Recognizing the importance of compound interest highlights the advantages of starting retirement savings early. It emphasizes the need to prioritize retirement contributions to maximize growth potential.

21.5 Creating a Retirement Plan

A well-structured retirement plan has several components:

- Establish a Savings Target: Based on your retirement goals and estimated expenses, determine how much you need to save each month. This target provides a clear benchmark for your savings efforts.
- Diversify Investments: Invest in a mix of assets to balance risk and growth potential. A diversified portfolio can help protect against market volatility and inflation.
- Review and Adjust: Regularly review your retirement plan and make adjustments based on changes in your financial situation, goals, or market conditions.

Explanation: Creating a comprehensive retirement plan allows individuals to take proactive steps toward achieving their retirement goals. It encourages regular monitoring and adjustments to stay on track.

Current Age	Retirement Age	Current Savings	Monthly Contribution	Expected Return (%)	Total at Retirement

To calculate the total savings at retirement, the Future Value (FV) formula is used. This accounts for the growth of both the initial savings and monthly contributions due to compound interest. Here's the formula:

Total Savings at Retirement Formula

The Future Value (FV) formula calculates the growth of initial savings and monthly contributions due to compound interest:
Formula:
$$FV = PV \times (1 + r)^n + PMT \times [(1 + r)^n - 1] / r$$
Where:
- FV = Future Value (total savings at retirement)
- PV = Present Value (current savings)
- r = Monthly interest rate (Annual Rate / 12)
- n = Total number of periods (months until retirement)
- PMT = Monthly contribution

Steps to Calculate:
1. Convert the annual return rate to a monthly rate:
2. r = (Expected Return %) / 100 / 12
3. Calculate the total number of months until retirement:
4. n = (Retirement Age - Current Age) × 12
5. Apply the formula in two parts:
   - Future value of current savings:
   - $FV_1 = PV \times (1 + r)^n$
   - Future value of monthly contributions:
   - $FV_2 = PMT \times [(1 + r)^n - 1] / r$
6. Combine both components to get the total future value:
7. $FV = FV_1 + FV_2$

This formula ensures the compounding effect of monthly contributions and initial savings is accounted for over the investment period. Would you like to explore more examples or details?

Comprehension
Q&A

Reflect on what you've learned in this chapter by answering the following questions.

Q1 Why is retirement planning essential for financial security?

Q2 What types of retirement accounts are available, and how do they differ?

Q3 Explain the benefits of starting retirement planning early.

Q4 Discuss various strategies for withdrawing funds during retirement.

Q5 Create a rough outline of your retirement plan, including your desired retirement age and savings goals.

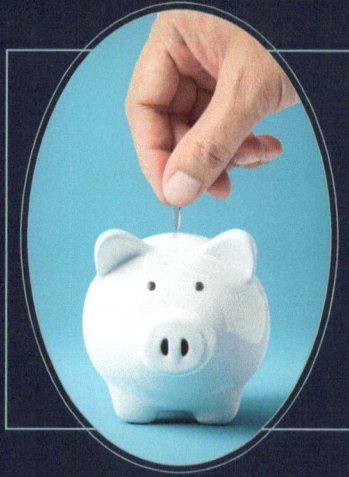

CHAPTER TWENTY-TWO
CONCLUSION

22.1 Recap of Key Concepts

The Personal Finance Handbook serves as a comprehensive resource for individuals seeking to enhance their financial literacy and achieve their financial goals. The chapters covered essential topics, including budgeting, saving, investing, debt management, and retirement planning. Each section provided valuable insights and practical tools to empower readers in their financial journeys.

22.2 Taking Control of Your Financial Future

By understanding and applying the concepts presented throughout this handbook, readers can take control of their financial future and build wealth over time. Financial literacy is the foundation for making informed decisions, setting achievable goals, and navigating the complexities of personal finance.

22.3 Continuous Learning and Adaptation

Personal finance is an evolving field, and staying informed about changes in financial products, tax laws, and market conditions is essential. Continuous learning and adaptation are critical to maintaining financial health and achieving long-term success.

22.4 Final Thoughts

The journey to financial security and independence requires dedication and commitment. By implementing the strategies and concepts outlined in this handbook, individuals can build a solid foundation for their financial future, achieve their goals, and enjoy the peace of mind that comes from being financially secure. May this book be the guide you need to reach your financial goals and shift from just surviving to thriving!

Setting Daily Financial
INTENTIONS

DAILY AFFIRMATIONS

....

....

TODAY I AM GRATEFUL FOR

....

....

TODAY'S TOP GOALS

01 ....

02 ....

03 ....

SCHEDULE

TIPS

REVIEW DAILY SPENDING LIMIT
- SET A REALISTIC SPENDING CAP FOR THE DAY TO STAY WITHIN YOUR BUDGET.

TRACK AND LOG EXPENSES
- RECORD EVERY EXPENSE, NO MATTER HOW SMALL, TO MAINTAIN AWARENESS OF YOUR SPENDING HABITS.

PRIORITIZE A FINANCIAL GOAL
- CHOOSE ONE FINANCIAL GOAL (E.G., SAVING, PAYING OFF DEBT) AND TAKE AT LEAST ONE SMALL ACTION TOWARD IT, SUCH AS TRANSFERRING MONEY TO SAVINGS OR SKIPPING A NON-ESSENTIAL PURCHASE.

FINAL THOUGHT

As you reach the end of this book, I hope the insights and strategies shared have resonated with you. Taking charge of your financial future is a journey, and every step you take brings you closer to your goals. Remember, it's not about perfection but about progress and making informed choices that align with your aspirations.

Stay committed, keep learning, and don't hesitate to seek guidance when needed. Your financial well-being is within your control, and with determination, you can build the future you envision. Here's to your successful financial journey ahead!

ABOUT THE AUTHORS

DR. NORMA MCLAUCHLIN,

Dr. N. McLauchlin is a financial expert with over 10 years of experience in personal finance, investment strategies, and financial education. Passionate about helping others achieve financial independence, She has authored several publications and conducted workshops on financial literacy and serves as both a literary and financial mentor for countless individuals nationally.

DELORIS TRAVIS

Deloris Travis is a dedicated and caring professional with a 20-year career in the United States Air Force, where she specialized in budget and finance. During her service, she ensured personnel were properly compensated, demonstrating her meticulous attention to detail and commitment to the well-being of others. Her military experience laid a strong foundation for her expertise in financial management and her passion for helping others.

After retiring from the Air Force, Deloris turned her focus to empowering individuals to take control of their finances. She is devoted to guiding others in creating effective budgets, achieving financial goals, and building a secure future. Known for her dedication and attention to detail, Deloris combines her financial expertise with her love of service to inspire and support those striving for financial success.

LINDA PARKER

Linda Parker is a trusted financial expert with over 20 years of service in the United States Army, where she excelled as a Traffic Management Coordinator and later as a Budget Technician. Her military career instilled in her a passion for financial management, discipline, and organizational excellence. Linda's lifelong dream of becoming an accountant led her to earn an MBA with a concentration in Accounting, fulfilling her love for numbers and helping others.

Driven by her desire to empower individuals, Linda helps people create and manage budgets, guiding them toward financial stability and success. An avid reader and enthusiastic traveler, she enjoys expanding her knowledge through books and exploring the beauty of nature through walking and hiking. Linda's blend of expertise, integrity, and care makes her a respected advisor and role model in her community.

*9 7 8 1 9 6 6 1 6 3 0 3 9 *